FUNCTIONAL FORM AND UTILITY

A Review of Consumer Demand Theory

UNDERGROUND CLASSICS IN ECONOMICS

Progress in economics takes place in many different forums. Many of these forums are not "above ground," in the sense of published work freely available. They are in the form of unpublished notes, dissertations, government reports, and lectures. This series is dedicated to making the best of this underground literature more widely available to libraries, scholars, and their students. In so doing it will serve to fill a large gap in the contemporary economic literature.

Entries in this series can be on any topic of interest to economists, and they may occasionally be in rough and sometimes unfinished form. The only criteria are that the works have been influential, widely cited, of exceptional excellence, and for whatever reason, never before published.

ABOUT THE BOOK AND AUTHOR

This is Professor Goldberger's classic survey of modern consumer demand theory. Consumer demand is a crucial component of any economy, and in this set of notes Professor Goldberger gives the theoretical base for which the composition of consumer expenditures is dependent upon income and prices.

Beginning with a review of classical demand theory, Goldberger first emphasizes the form of utility and demand functions, then gradually specializes the theory to accommodate the linear expenditure system and alternative specifications of complete sets of demand functions. Empirical consequences of the theory are highlighted throughout.

This widely cited and justly influential study is being published for the first time. This significant document in recent economic theory will be useful to scholars seeking to understand not only what we know about consumer demand theory but also how we came to know it.

Arthur S. Goldberger is Vilas Research Professor of Economics, University of Wisconsin-Madison.

FUNCTIONAL FORM AND UTILITY

A Review of Consumer Demand Theory

ARTHUR S. GOLDBERGER

WESTVIEW PRESS / BOULDER AND LONDON

Underground Classics in Economics

This Westview softcover edition is printed on acid-free paper and bound in softcovers that carry the highest rating of the National Association of State Textbook Administrators, in consultation with the Association of American Publishers and the Book Manufacturers' Institute.

Published in 1987 in the United States of America by Westview Press, Inc.; Frederick A. Praeger, Publisher; 5500 Central Avenue, Boulder, Colorado 80301

Library of Congress Cataloging-in-Publication Data
Goldberger, Arthur Stanley, 1930-
Functional form and utility.
(Underground classics in economics)
Bibliography: p.
1. Consumption (Economics) I. Title. II. Series.
HB820.G65 1987 339.4'7 87-28046
ISBN 0-8133-7489-8

Printed and bound in the United States of America

The paper used in this publication meets the requirements of the American National Standard for Permanence of Paper for Printed Library Materials Z39.48-1984.

6 5 4 3 2

For Nina and Nick

CONTENTS

PREFACE

During a year's leave (1964-65) at the Center for Planning and Economic Research in Athens, I began working with consumer expenditure data, as a building block for a planned macroeconometric model of Greece. While the model never materialized, I brought back to Wisconsin an interest in systems of demand equations, and also my research assistant, Theodore Gamaletsos. Stimulated by Richard Stone's work, and by the availability of consistent national accounts for a number of countries, we decided to prepare an international comparison using time series data.

I thought it worthwhile to review the relevant literature in conjunction with that empirical task. The review grew into this essay, completed in October 1967. It was issued in mimeographed form as "Functional form and utility: a review of consumer demand theory", Systems Formulation, Methodology, and Policy Workshop Paper 6703, by the Social Systems Research Institute, University of Wisconsin. In that form, it was widely circulated and widely cited.

Our own empirical project, completed in 1967, was eventually published: Goldberger and Gamaletsos (1970). Further analyses, including additional functional forms and an updated data base, were undertaken by Gamaletsos in his doctoral dissertation, which was subsequently summarized as

T. Gamaletsos (1973), "Further analysis of cross-country comparison of consumer expenditure patterns," European Economic Review, Vol. 4, pp. 1-20.

To this day, I get occasional requests for a copy of my essay. Perhaps the comprehensive coverage, uniformity of notation, and detailed derivations have made it useful to several cohorts of students. Or perhaps its relative scarcity has made it seem valuable.

In editing it for publication now, I've made only minor changes -- removing old typographical errors, and citing the published rather than unpublished versions of several papers. I should add that Antonius Barten's (1966) Dutch dissertation, on which I drew heavily, was summarized in

A. P. Barten (1968), "Estimating demand equations," Econometrica, Vol. 36, April, pp. 213-251.

In the years around 1970, consumer demand analysis was a very active research field. Many of the contemporary developments, including the incorporation of savings and the refinement of estimation methods, are well documented in the book

A. A. Powell (1974), Empirical Analytics of Demand Systems, Lexington, Mass: D. C. Heath and Company.

A rich picture of the broad field of consumer economics at about the same time is to be found in

A. Brown and A. Deaton (1977), "Models of consumer behaviour: a survey," Economic Journal, Vol. 82, pp. 1145-1236.

In the intervening years, the subject was revolutionized, in part by the application of duality theory. A modern view, which also shows how the principles extend into many other areas of economics is provided in the authoritative text

A. Deaton and J. Muellbauer (1980), Economics and Consumer Behavior, Cambridge: Cambridge University Press.

Since 1970, I've done little work on consumer demand systems, but some lessons learned there did show up in my work on multivariate regression and latent-variable models.

My original research was supported in part by grants from the Graduate School of the University of Wisconsin, and I was helped also by comments of Gerard Adams, De Ray Norton, Guy Orcutt, and Harold Watts. In 1967 Alice Wilcox typed the Social Systems Research Institute workshop paper. In 1987 she typed this version. The technology has changed, but the requirements were just as demanding on this round. For her expert and cheerful help, I am extremely grateful.

Arthur S. Goldberger

1
INTRODUCTION

The most casual examination of data reveals wide variation across countries and across time in the composition of consumer expenditures. To what extent can this variation be accounted for by variation in observable determinants? To what extent must we fall back on variations in tastes? In a forthcoming paper, Goldberger and Gamaletsos (1970) undertake a cross-country comparison of consumer expenditure patterns with such questions in mind.

We approach the problem by estimating, for each of 13 countries, a "complete set" of 5 consumer demand functions. A "complete set of consumer demand functions" is one in which the quantity demanded of each of n goods is determined as a function of total consumer expenditure and the prices of the n goods. In the empirical work we give primary attention to the linear expenditure system introduced by Stone (1954). Our data base consists of short annual time series drawn from the national accounts of the Organization for Economic Cooperation and Development (OECD). Earlier versions of this data base were used by Houthakker (1960b, 1965a) to estimate constant elasticity and indirect-addilog systems of demand functions. Our motivation for analyzing the data is similar to that indicated by Houthakker, whose 1960 paper begins, "Both for the scientific study of economic development and for the rational formulation of economic policy it is important to obtain concise and realistic descriptions of the behavior of household consumption under varying conditions." Some comparison of our results will therefore be of interest.

Any attempt to estimate a complete set of demand functions from short time series must rely heavily on extraneous information. Each of the n equations presumably requires one parameter for the total expenditure variable and n parameters for the n price variables; the complete set would thus require $n(n + 1)$ parameters. Even with $n = 5$, few degrees of freedom would remain in short time series. As is customary in studies of consumer expenditure patterns, we will be looking to the classical theory of consumer demand for extraneous information.

The present paper is intended to provide a theoretical base for our empirical work. Classical consumer demand theory is reviewed, emphasis being put on the form of utility and demand functions. The theory is developed in general terms in Chapter 2, with reference to the linear expenditure system in Chapter 3, and with reference to alternative specifications of complete sets of demand functions in Chapter 4. Some summary remarks are offered in Chapter 5.

This entire paper draws heavily on work of Barten, Theil, Houthakker, and Stone and is little, if any, more than a gloss on selected portions of their contributions.

2
CLASSICAL CONSUMER DEMAND THEORY

2.1 Derivation of Complete Set of Demand Functions

We begin by restating the classical theory of consumer demand, adopting the convenient matrix notation introduced by Barten (1964) and Theil (1965) and developed further in Barten (1966, Chapters 1 and 2) and Theil (1967, Chapter 6).

Let q_i denote the quantity purchased of good i (i = 1, ... n), p_i denote the price of good i (i = 1,...,n), and y denote income. All these variables are positive. We define the n x 1 quantity vector q and the n x 1 price vector p by

$$q = (q_1,\ldots,q_n)' \qquad p = (p_1,\ldots,p_n)'.$$

Given p and y, the consumer selects q to maximize the value of his utility function

$$u = u(q)$$

subject to the budget constraint

$$p'q = y.$$

The utility function will have certain classical properties. First, it is repeatedly differentiable. Denote the first derivatives (the marginal utilities of the goods) by $u_i = \partial u/\partial q_i$ (i = 1,...,n), and the second derivatives by $u_{ij} = \partial u_i/\partial q_j = \partial^2 u/\partial q_i\, \partial q_j$,

$(i,j = 1,\ldots,n)$. We define the $n \times 1$ marginal utility vector u_q by

$$u_q = \partial u/\partial q = (u_1,\ldots,u_n)'$$

and the $n \times n$ second derivative matrix U by

$$U = \partial u_q/\partial q' = \begin{pmatrix} u_{11} & \cdots & u_{1n} \\ \vdots & & \vdots \\ u_{n1} & \cdots & u_{nn} \end{pmatrix} .$$

It will be assumed that $u_i > 0$ $(i=1,\ldots,n)$, so that marginal utilities are everywhere positive. Further it will be assumed that the symmetric matrix U is negative definite everywhere. While not necessary, this assumption ensures that the constrained maximum problem has a unique solution for q as a function of y and p, an assurance that we shall rely on. (Incidentally, it implies $u_{ii} < 0$ $(i=1,\ldots,n)$ so that there is diminishing marginal utility to each good.)

The constrained maximization of $u = u(q)$ subject to $y = p'q$ may be carried out with the aid of the Lagrangian multiplier. Thus we consider

$$\bar{u}(q, \lambda) = u(q) - \lambda(p'q - y)$$

where λ is the Lagrangian multiplier, and choose q and λ to locate the extremum of $\bar{u}(q,\lambda)$ without constraint. Differentiating with respect to q gives

$$\bar{u}_q = \partial\bar{u}/\partial q = u_q - \lambda\, p,$$

while differentiating with respect to λ gives

$$\bar{u}_\lambda = \partial\bar{u}/\partial\lambda = -(p'q - y).$$

When these derivatives are set equal to zero we find

$$(2.1) \quad u_q = \lambda\, p \, , \qquad p'q = y$$

which are the familiar set of $n + 1$ first order conditions in the $n + 1$ unknowns of q and λ. That these conditions locate a maximum is ensured by the negative definiteness of U, which further guarantees that (2.1) may be solved uniquely for q and λ as functions of y and p. We denote the solution as

$$q = q(y, p), \qquad \lambda = \lambda(y, p).$$

The n equations of $q = q(y, p)$, namely

$$q_i = q_i(y, p) = q_i(y, p_1,\ldots,p_n) \quad (i = 1,\ldots,n)$$

constitute the complete set of consumer demand functions. Each equation in the set gives the quantity demanded of one of the goods as a function of income and all prices. This set of demand functions is the main target of the classical theory of consumer demand. When a particular functional form for $u = u(q)$ is specified, then one may be able to obtain the explicit functional form for $q = q(y,p)$, the parameters of the latter being related to those of the former.

In the spirit of generality which characterizes the classical approach, however, it is possible to proceed without specifying a particular utility function. General features can be identified which the differentials of $q = q(y, p)$ and $\lambda(y, p)$ will possess regardless of the specifics of $u = u(q)$.

Consider the ith demand function $q_i = q_i(y,p)$; its slope with respect to income is $\partial q_i/\partial y$, and its slopes with respect to prices are $\partial q_i/\partial p_j$ $(j = 1,\ldots,n)$. Similarly the function $\lambda = \lambda(y, p)$ has income slope $\partial\lambda/\partial y$ and price slopes $\partial\lambda/\partial p_j$ $(j = 1,\ldots,n)$. All of these slopes may be collected into a compact form. For the set of demand functions $q = q(y, p)$ we define the n x 1 income slope vector q_y by

$$q_y = \partial q/\partial y = (\partial q_1/\partial y,\ldots,\partial q_n/\partial y)'$$

and the n x n price slope matrix Q_p -- Cournot price slope matrix in the terminology of Frisch (1959, p. 179) -- by

$$Q_p = \partial q/\partial p' = \begin{pmatrix} \partial q_1/\partial p_1 & \cdots & \partial q_1/\partial p_n \\ \vdots & & \vdots \\ \partial q_n/\partial p_1 & \cdots & \partial q_n/\partial p_n \end{pmatrix}.$$

Similarly for $\lambda = \lambda(y, p)$ we define the (scalar) income slope λ_y by

$$\lambda_y = \partial\lambda/\partial y$$

and the n x 1 price slope vector λ_p by

$$\lambda_p = \partial\lambda/\partial p = (\partial\lambda/\partial p_1, \ldots, \partial\lambda/\partial p_n)'.$$

We further introduce the differential dy and the differential vectors dp and dq where

$$dp = (dp_1,\ldots,dp_n)' \qquad dq = (dq_1,\ldots,dq_n)'.$$

With this notation the total differentials of $q = q(y, p)$ and $\lambda = \lambda(y,p)$ are expressed as

$$\text{(2.2a)} \qquad dq = q_y\,dy + Q_p\,dp \qquad d\lambda = \lambda_y\,dy + \lambda_p'dp,$$

or still more compactly in

$$\text{(2.3)} \qquad \begin{pmatrix} dq \\ -d\lambda \end{pmatrix} = \begin{pmatrix} q_y & Q_p \\ -\lambda_y & -\lambda_p' \end{pmatrix} \begin{pmatrix} dy \\ dp \end{pmatrix}.$$

The total differentials of the first-order conditions $u_q = \lambda p$ and $p'q = y$ are similarly expressed as

$$U\,dq = p\,d\lambda + \lambda\,dp \qquad dy = p'dq + q'dp,$$

or more compactly in

$$\text{(2.4)} \qquad \begin{pmatrix} U & p \\ p' & 0 \end{pmatrix} \begin{pmatrix} dq \\ -d\lambda \end{pmatrix} = \begin{pmatrix} 0 & \lambda I \\ 1 & -q' \end{pmatrix} \begin{pmatrix} dy \\ dp \end{pmatrix},$$

an expression which Barten (1966, p. 17) calls the "fundamental matrix equation of the theory of consumer demand in terms of infinitesimal changes."

Since both (2.3) and (2.4) hold for arbitrary dy, dp, we find

$$\text{(2.5)} \qquad \begin{pmatrix} U & p \\ p' & 0 \end{pmatrix} \begin{pmatrix} q_y & Q_p \\ -\lambda_y & -\lambda_p' \end{pmatrix} = \begin{pmatrix} 0 & \lambda I \\ 1 & -q' \end{pmatrix}$$

-- the "fundamental matrix equation of the theory of consumer demand in terms of partial derivatives," Barten (1966, p. 18). It is (2.5) which, in conjunction with $p'q = y$, permits us to deduce general features which a complete set of demand functions will possess regardless of the underlying utility function.

The inverse of the first matrix on the left of (2.5) is

$$\begin{pmatrix} U & p \\ p' & 0 \end{pmatrix}^{-1} = (p'U^{-1}p)^{-1} \begin{bmatrix} (p'U^{-1}p)U^{-1} - (U^{-1}p)(U^{-1}p)' & U^{-1}p \\ (U^{-1}p)' & -1 \end{bmatrix}$$

Thus the solution of (2.5) for the slopes is (2.6):

$$\begin{pmatrix} q_y & Q_p \\ -\lambda_y & -\lambda_p' \end{pmatrix} = (p'U^{-1}p)^{-1} \begin{pmatrix} U^{-1}p & (p'U^{-1}p)\lambda U^{-1} - \lambda(U^{-1}p)(U^{-1}p)' - U^{-1}pq' \\ -1 & \lambda(U^{-1}p)' + q' \end{pmatrix}$$

the blocks of which may be read off clockwise as

(2.7) $\lambda_y = (p'U^{-1}p)^{-1}$

(2.8) $q_y = \lambda_y U^{-1}p$

(2.9) $Q_p = \lambda U^{-1} - \lambda \lambda_y (U^{-1}p)(U^{-1}p)' - \lambda_y U^{-1}p q'$

(2.10) $\lambda_p = -\lambda_y(\lambda U^{-1}p + q)$.

For most purposes, it is useful to substitute (2.8) into (2.9) and (2.10); in this version the solutions are

(2.11) $\lambda_y = (p'U^{-1}p)^{-1}$

(2.12) $\lambda_p = -(\lambda q_y + \lambda_y q)$

(2.13) $q_y = \lambda_y U^{-1}p$

(2.14) $Q_p = \lambda U^{-1} - \lambda \lambda_y^{-1} q_y q_y' - q_y q'$.

The general features of the complete set of demand functions are now obtainable. We borrow the terminology of Frisch (1959, p. 180) in naming them. Premultiplying (2.13) through by p' gives the "Engel aggregation" condition

$$p'q_y = \lambda_y \, p'U^{-1}p = 1 \tag{2.15a}$$

in view of (2.11). Algebraically

$$\textstyle\sum_i p_i(\partial q_i/\partial y) = 1.$$

Postmultiplying the transpose of (2.14) through by p gives the "Cournot aggregation" condition

$$Q_p' \, p = \lambda \, U^{-1}p - \lambda \, \lambda_y^{-1}q_y \, q_y' \, p - q \, q_y' \, p$$

$$= \lambda \, \lambda_y^{-1}q_y - \lambda \, \lambda_y^{-1}q_y - q$$

$$= - q \tag{2.16a}$$

in view of (2.13), (2.15a), and the symmetry of U^{-1}. Algebraically

$$\textstyle\sum_i p_i(\partial q_i/\partial p_j) = -q_j \qquad (j = 1, \ldots, n).$$

Since U^{-1} is symmetric, so is $\lambda \, U^{-1} - \lambda \, \lambda_y^{-1}q_y q_y'$, so that we find the "symmetry" condition

$$(Q_p + q_y \, q')' = (Q_p + q_y \, q'), \tag{2.17a}$$

in view of (2.14). Algebraically

$$(\partial q_i/\partial p_j) + (\partial q_i/\partial y) \, q_j = (\partial q_j/\partial p_i) + (\partial q_j/\partial y) \, q_i \qquad (i,j = 1, \ldots, n).$$

Equations (2.15a), (2.16a), (2.17a) comprise the main content of the classical theory. They indicate <u>restrictions</u> connecting income and price slopes which any complete set of demand functions must possess if it is derivable from maximization of any utility function of the broad class being considered here. They therefore indicate the substantial economies in parameterizing a complete set of demand functions that are made available when a classical utility maximization process is postulated.

Another familiar equation follows directly from the others and the budget constraint, and hence imposes no further restrictions. Postmultiplying (2.17a) through by p gives

$$Q_p\ p + q_y\ q'p = Q_p'\ p + q\ q_y'\ p = -\ q + q = 0$$

in view of (2.16a) and (2.15a). Since $q'p = y$, we find the "homogeneity condition"

$$(2.18a)\quad Q_p\ p = -\ q_y\ y.$$

Algebraically

$$\textstyle\sum_j(\partial q_i/\partial p_j)p_j = -\ (\partial q_i/\partial y)y \qquad (i = 1,\ \ldots,\ n).$$

Economists are accustomed to thinking in terms of elasticities rather than slopes so that it will be useful to restate the results in those terms. Consider the i<u>th</u> demand function $q_i = q_i(y,\ p)$; its elasticity with respect to income is $\eta_i = (\partial q_i/\partial y)(y/q_i)$, and its elasticities with respect to prices are $\eta_{ij} = (\partial q_i/\partial p_j)(p_j/q_i)$ $(j = 1,\ \ldots,\ n)$. All of these elasticities may be collected into a compact form. For the set of demand functions $q = q(y,\ p)$ we define the n x 1 income elasticity vector η by

$$\eta = (\eta_1,\ \ldots,\ \eta_n)'$$

and the n x n price elasticity matrix H by

$$H = \begin{pmatrix} \eta_{11} & \cdots & \eta_{1n} \\ \vdots & & \vdots \\ \eta_{n1} & \cdots & \eta_{nn} \end{pmatrix}.$$

Direct definitions of η and H become available if we define the n x n diagonal matrices of prices and quantities,

$$\hat{p} = \begin{pmatrix} p_1 & 0 & \dots & 0 \\ 0 & p_2 & \dots & 0 \\ \cdot & \cdot & & \cdot \\ \cdot & \cdot & & \cdot \\ \cdot & \cdot & & \cdot \\ 0 & 0 & \dots & p_n \end{pmatrix} \qquad \hat{q} = \begin{pmatrix} q_1 & 0 & \dots & 0 \\ 0 & q_2 & \dots & 0 \\ \cdot & \cdot & & \cdot \\ \cdot & \cdot & & \cdot \\ \cdot & \cdot & & \cdot \\ 0 & 0 & \dots & q_n \end{pmatrix}.$$

For it is readily confirmed that

$$\eta = y\,\hat{q}^{-1} q_y \quad , \qquad H = \hat{q}^{-1} Q_p\, \hat{p}.$$ [1]

Now the total differential of $q = q(y, p)$, namely

(2.2a) $$dq = q_y\, dy + Q_p\, dp,$$

may be re-expressed in terms of logarithmic differentials and elasticities as

(2.2b) $$d\log q = \eta\, (d\log y) + H\, (d\log p).$$

For premultiplying (2.2a) through by $\hat{q}^{-1}$ gives

$$\begin{aligned} \hat{q}^{-1} dq &= \hat{q}^{-1} q_y\, dy + \hat{q}^{-1} Q_p\, dp = \\ &= (\hat{q}^{-1} q_y\, y)(y^{-1} dy) + (\hat{q}^{-1}\, Q_p\, \hat{p})(\hat{p}^{-1} dp) \end{aligned}$$

which is just (2.2b).

To proceed, we denote the <u>average budget shares</u> by

$$w_i = p_i q_i / y \qquad\qquad (i = 1, \dots n);$$

they measure the proportions of income spent on the n goods. These may be collected into the n x 1 average budget share vector w, defined by

$$w = (w_1, \dots, w_n)'.$$

A direct definition of w is

$$w = y^{-1} \hat{p}\, q = y^{-1} \hat{q}\, p.$$

These budget shares sum to unity:

$$\iota' w = \iota' y^{-1} \hat{p} \, q = y^{-1} \, \iota' \hat{p} \, q = y^{-1} p' q = 1$$

in view of $p'q = y$; here

$$\iota = (1, \ldots, 1)'$$

denotes the n x 1 "summer" vector, all of whose elements are 1.

Now the classical restrictions may be expressed in terms of the elasticities of the demand functions, that is in terms of the coefficients in (2.2b). First, Engel aggregation is shown by

$$\text{(2.15b)} \quad w' \eta = (y^{-1} p' \hat{q})(y \, \hat{q}^{-1} q_y) = p' q_y = 1$$

in view of (2.15a). Algebraically

$$\sum_i w_i \, \eta_i = 1.$$

Second, Cournot aggregation is shown by

$$H' w = (\hat{p} \, Q_p' \, \hat{q}^{-1})(y^{-1} \, \hat{q} \, p) = y^{-1} \, \hat{p} \, Q_p' \, p = y^{-1} \, \hat{p}(-q)$$

$$\text{(2.16b)} \qquad = - w$$

in view of (2.16a). Algebraically

$$\sum_i w_i \, \eta_{ij} = - w_j \qquad (j = 1, \ldots, n).$$

Third, symmetry is manifested in

$$[\hat{w}(H + \eta \, w')]' = (H' + w \, \eta')\hat{w}$$

$$= [\hat{p} Q_p' \hat{q}^{-1} + (y^{-1} \hat{p} \, q)(y q_y' \hat{q}^{-1})](y^{-1} \hat{q} \, \hat{p})$$

$$= y^{-1} \hat{p}(Q_p' + q \, q_y')\hat{p} = y^{-1} \hat{p}(Q_p + q_y \, q')\hat{p}$$

$$\text{(2.17b)} \qquad = \hat{w} \, (H + \eta \, w')$$

in view of (2.17a). Algebraically

$$w_i(\eta_{ij} + \eta_i\, w_j) = w_j(\eta_{ji} + \eta_j\, w_i) \quad (i,j = 1,\dots,n).$$

The homogeneity condition again follows. Postmultiply (2.17b) through by ι; this gives

$$\hat{w}(H\,\iota + \eta\, w'\iota) = H'w + w\,\eta'w = H'w + w = 0$$

in view of $\hat{w}\,\iota = w$, (2.16b), and (2.15b). Then since $w'\iota = 1$,

(2.18b) $H\,\iota = -\,\eta.$

Algebraically

$$\textstyle\sum_j \eta_{ij} = -\,\eta_i \qquad (i = 1, \dots, n).$$

Economists are also accustomed to thinking in terms of the average budget shares rather than the quantities or the logarithms of quantities so that another restatement of results may be useful. Let us premultiply (2.2a) through by $y^{-1}\hat{p}$, or equivalently (2.2b) by $\hat{w}$. We find

$$y^{-1}\hat{p}\;dq = y^{-1}\hat{p}\;q_y\;dy + y^{-1}\hat{p}\;Q_p\;dp$$

or

$$y^{-1}\hat{p}\;\hat{q}\;\hat{q}^{-1}dq = \hat{p}\;q_y\;y^{-1}dy + y^{-1}\hat{p}\;Q_p\;\hat{p}\;\hat{p}^{-1}dp.$$

This may be written as

(2.2c) $\hat{w}\;\mathrm{dlog}\;q = \mu\;\mathrm{dlog}\;y + \theta\;\mathrm{dlog}\;p$

where we have defined the n x 1 marginal budget share vector μ by

$$\mu = (\mu_1, \dots, \mu_n)' = \hat{p}\;q_y = \hat{w}\;\eta$$

and the n x n price response matrix θ by

$$\theta = \begin{pmatrix} \theta_{11} & \cdots & \theta_{1n} \\ \vdots & & \\ \theta_{n1} & \cdots & \theta_{nn} \end{pmatrix} = y^{-1}\;\hat{p}\;Q_p\;\hat{p} = \hat{w}\;H.$$

The motivation for this transformation runs as follows. Algebraically, (2.2c) says that

$$w_i \,\text{dlog}\, q_i = \mu_i \,\text{dlog}\, y + \sum_j \theta_{ij} \,\text{dlog}\, p_j \quad (i=1,\ldots,n)$$

where

$$\mu_i = y^{-1} p_i (\partial q_i/\partial y) = w_i \eta_i \qquad (i=1,\ldots,n)$$

and

$$\theta_{ij} = y^{-1} p_i p_j (\partial q_i/\partial p_j) = w_i \eta_{ij} \qquad (i,j=1,\ldots,n).$$

The μ_i's measure the proportions of incremental income spent on the n goods, prices being given. The left-hand variable w_i dlog q_i has the following interpretation: Consider the total differential of the ith average budget share:

$$dw_i = d(p_i q_i/y) = (q_i/y)dp_i + (p_i/y)dq_i - (p_i q_i/y^2)dy$$

$$= (p_i q_i/y)(dp_i/p_i) + (p_i q_i/y)(dq_i/q_i)$$

$$- (p_i q_i/y)(dy/y)$$

(2.19) $$= w_i \,\text{dlog}\, p_i + w_i \,\text{dlog}\, q_i - w_i \,\text{dlog}\, y.$$

In many contexts, primary interest attaches to changes in the average budget shares, w_i, in response to changes in income and prices. As we see from (2.19), w_i dlog q_i is just the "endogenous component" of dw_i, the one over which the consumer exercises choice. It therefore seems plausible to treat the w_i dlog q_i as the dependent variables as is done in (2.2c), rather than treat the dq_i or the dlog q_i as dependent variables as was done in (2.2a) and (2.2b), respectively. Theil (1967, pp. 182-183), in making this point, refers to w_i dlog q_i as "the quantity component of the change in the ith value [i.e., average budget] share."

The classical restrictions may be expressed again in terms of the coefficients in (2.2c). First, Engel aggregation is shown by

(2.15c) $$\iota'\mu = \iota'\hat{w}\,\eta = w'\eta = 1$$

in view of (2.15b). Algebraically

$$\sum_i \mu_i = 1.$$

Cournot aggregation is shown by

$$(2.16c)\quad \theta'\iota = H'\hat{w}\,\iota = H'w = -w$$

in view of (2.16b). Algebraically

$$\sum_i \theta_{ij} = -w_j \qquad (j = 1, \ldots, n).$$

Symmetry is shown by

$$(2.17c)\quad (\theta + \mu\, w')' = [\hat{w}(H+\eta\, w')]' = \hat{w}(H+\eta\, w') = \theta + \mu\, w'$$

in view of (2.17b). Algebraically

$$\theta_{ij} + \mu_i\, w_j = \theta_{ji} + \mu_j\, w_i \qquad (i,\, j = 1, \ldots, n).$$

Homogeneity is shown by

$$(2.18c)\quad \theta\,\iota = \hat{w}\,H\,\iota = -\hat{w}\,\eta = -\mu$$

in view of (2.18b). Algebraically

$$\sum_j \theta_{ij} = -\mu_i \qquad (i = 1, \ldots, n).$$

2.2 Utility Aspects of the Demand Functions

We proceed to some utility aspects of the classical theory, again following the lead of Barten and Theil.

The demand functions $q = q(y, p)$ may be inserted into the utility function $u = u(q)$ to give maximum attainable utility as a function of y and p:

$$u = u(q(y, p)) = u^*(y, p),$$

say. The function $u^*(y, p)$ is the <u>indirect</u> utility function as distinguished from the <u>direct</u> utility function $u = u(q)$. The slope of the indirect utility function with respect to income is $\partial u^*/\partial y$, and its slopes with respect to prices are $\partial u^*/\partial p_j$ $(j = 1, \ldots, n)$. We express these, in the spirit of the notation used earlier, as

$$u^*_y = \partial u^*/\partial y, \quad u^*_p = \partial u^*/\partial p = (\partial u^*/\partial p_1, \ldots, \partial u^*/\partial p_n)'.$$

Applying the chain rule for differentiation, we have

$$u^*_y = u'_q\, q_y \qquad\qquad u^{*\prime}_p = u'_q\, Q_p$$

which by virtue of the first order condition $u_q = \lambda\, p$ imply

$$u^*_y = \lambda\, p'q_y \qquad\qquad u^{*\prime}_p = \lambda\, p'\, Q_p\ ,$$

which in turn imply

$$(2.20) \qquad u^*_y = \lambda \qquad\qquad u^*_p = -\,\lambda\, q$$

since

$$p'q_y = 1 \text{ and } p'Q_p = -\,q'.$$

The Lagrangian multiplier λ has now been identified as the marginal utility of income, so that the function $\lambda = \lambda(y,\, p)$ gives the marginal utility of income as a function of income and prices. Thus, the slope of the marginal utility of income with respect to income is λ_y and the vector of its slopes with respect to prices is λ_p. It will be convenient to denote the <u>income elasticity of the marginal utility of income</u> by

$$\eta_{\lambda y} = (\partial\lambda/\partial y)(y/\lambda) = \lambda_y\, \lambda^{-1} y$$

and its reciprocal, the <u>income flexibility</u>, by

$$\phi = 1/\eta_{\lambda y} = \lambda_y^{-1}\lambda\, y^{-1}.\ ^2$$

We shall have frequent occasion to replace $\lambda_y^{-1}\lambda$ by its equivalent, $\phi\, y$. The marginal utility of income is positive, but declines with income: since u_q and p are positive, $u_q = \lambda\, p$ shows that λ is positive; since U is negative definite, so is U^{-1}, whence $\lambda_y = (p'U^{-1}p)^{-1}$ is negative; it then follows that

$\eta_{\lambda y} < 0$ $\phi < 0.$

The total differential of $u = u^*(y, p)$ is

$$du = u^*_y\, dy + u^{*\prime}_p\, dp = \lambda\, dy - \lambda\, q'dp = \lambda\, (dy - q'dp)$$

using (2.20). The total differential of $\lambda = \lambda(y, p)$ is

$$d\lambda = \lambda_y\, dy + \lambda_p'\, dp = \lambda_y\, dy - (\lambda\, q_y + \lambda_y\, q)'\, dp$$

using (2.12). Setting $du = 0$ gives the income change

$$(dy)^* = q'dp$$

which will, in the small, compensate for a price change dp, in the sense of keeping <u>utility</u> unchanged. Alternatively, setting $d\lambda = 0$ gives the income change

$$(dy)^{**} = (\lambda\, \lambda_y^{-1}\, q_y + q)'\, dp = (\phi\, y\, q_y + q)'\, dp$$

which will, in the small, compensate for a price change dp, in the sense of keeping the <u>marginal utility of income</u> unchanged.

With these two concepts of compensation in hand, two decompositions of the effects of price changes upon quantities demanded are possible. Recall that the total differential of the demand functions $q = q(y, p)$ is

$$dq = q_y\, dy + Q_p\, dp = q_y\, dy + (\lambda\, U^{-1} - \lambda\, \lambda_y^{-1} q_y\, q_y' - q_y\, q')dp.$$

Given a price change dp, suppose that is accompanied by an income change $dy = (dy)^* = q'dp$. The response to such a <u>utility-compensated</u> price change is seen to be

$$(dq)^* = q_y(q'\, dp) + Q_p\, dp = (Q_p + q_y\, q')\, dp = Q^*_p\, dp,$$

say, where

$$Q^*_p = Q_p + q_y\, q' = \lambda\, U^{-1} - \lambda\, \lambda_y^{-1}\, q_y\, q_y' = \lambda\, U^{-1} - \phi\, y\, q_y\, q_y'.$$

The symmetric matrix Q_p^* may be referred to as the utility-compensated (or Slutsky) price slope matrix of the demand functions. Its i,j element

$$(\partial q_i/\partial p_j)^* = (\partial q_i/\partial p_j) + (\partial q_i/\partial y)q_j$$
$$= \lambda\ u^{ij} - \phi\ y\ (\partial q_i/\partial y)(\partial q_j/\partial y)$$

measures the response of the quantity demanded of the i<u>th</u> good to a change in the price of the j<u>th</u> good when that price change is accompanied by an income change which just maintains utility. The total effect of a price change, $(\partial q_i/\partial p_j)$, has thus been decomposed into a substitution effect, $(\partial q_i/\partial p_j)^*$, and an income effect, $- (\partial q_i/\partial y)q_j$. On the Hicks-Allen definition, goods i and j are classified as substitutes, independent, or complements according as $(\partial q_i/\partial p_j)^* = (\partial q_j/\partial p_i)^*$ is positive, zero, or negative.

Alternatively, given a price change dp, suppose that it is accompanied by an income change $dy = (dy)^{**} = (\phi\ y\ q_y + q)'dp$. The response to such a <u>marginal-utility-of-income-compensated</u> price change is seen to be

$$(dq)^{**} = q_y\ (\phi\ y\ q_y + q)'dp + Q_p\ dp =$$
$$= (Q_p + q_y\ q' + \phi\ y\ q_y\ q_y')\ dp$$
$$= Q_p^{**}\ dp,$$

say, where

$$Q_p^{**} = (Q_p + q_y\ q' + \phi\ y\ q_y\ q_y') = (Q_p^* + \phi\ y\ q_y\ q_y') =$$
$$= \lambda\ U^{-1}.$$

The symmetric matrix Q_p^{**} may be referred to as the marginal-utility-of-income-compensated (or Frisch[3]) price slope matrix of the demand functions. Its i, j element

$$(\partial q_i/\partial p_j)^{**} = (\partial q_i/\partial p_j) + (\partial q_i/\partial y)\, q_j + \phi\, y\, (\partial q_i/\partial y)(\partial q_j/\partial y)$$
$$= (\partial q_i/\partial p_j)^{*} + \phi\, y\, (\partial q_i/\partial y)(\partial q_j/\partial y)$$
$$= \lambda\, u^{ij}$$

(where u^{ij} denotes the i, j element of U^{-1}), measures the response of the quantity demanded of the i<u>th</u> good in response to a change in the price of the j<u>th</u> good when that price change is accompanied by an income change which just maintains the marginal utility of income. The total effect of an uncompensated price change, $(\partial q_i/\partial p_j)$, has thus been decomposed into three terms: a specific substitution effect $(\partial q_i/\partial p_j)^{**}$, a general substitution effect $(\partial q_i/\partial p_j)^{*} - (\partial q_i/\partial p_j)^{**}$, and an income effect $-(\partial q_i/\partial y)q_j$. On a definition suggested by a passage in Houthakker (1960a, p. 248), goods i and j might be reclassified as substitutes, independent, or complements according as $(\partial q_i/\partial p_j)^{**} = (\partial q_j/\partial p_i)^{**}$ is positive, zero, or negative; that is, according as $u^{ij} = u^{ji} \gtreqless 0$.

Schematically, the decompositions are indicated as:

$Q_p =$	$\lambda\ U^{-1}$	$-\phi\ y\ q_y\ q_y'$	$-q_y\ q'$
Total effect	Specific substitution effect	General substitution effect	Income effect
	Substitution effect	Substitution effect	

It is now instructive to consider the demand functions in terms of Q_p^{*} and Q_p^{**}. The total differential of the demand functions, originally expressed as

$$(2.2a) \qquad dq = q_y\, dy + Q_p\, dp,$$

may in view of the definitions of Q_p^* and Q_p^{**} alternatively be expressed as

$$(2.2d) \qquad dq = q_y\, (dy - q'dp) + Q_p^*\, dp$$

or as

$$dq = q_y\, (dy - \phi\, y\, q_y'\, dp - q'dp) + Q_p^{**}\, dp$$

$$(2.2e) \qquad = q_y\, (dy - q'dp) + Q_p^{**}\, (dp - p\, q_y'dp)$$

-- the last equality sign being based on the fact that $Q_p^{**}p = \phi\, y\, q_y$, as shown in (2.18e) below. While in (2.2a) q_y is the coefficient of the change in nominal income, in (2.2d) and (2.2e) it is the coefficient of the change in a deflated income variable. While in (2.2a) and (2.2d) the last term refers to changes in nominal prices, in (2.2e) it refers to changes in deflated prices. Note that $q'dp = (dy)^*$ is the income change required to maintain utility, in the small, in the face of the price change dp. This means that q'dp gives, in the small, the change in a true cost of living index, so that (dy - q'dp) gives, in the small, the change in real income. A parallel interpretation in terms of maintaining marginal utility of income may be made for the deflated price terms. For a brief discussion of deflation of the kind being considered here and in the sequel, see Theil (1964, pp. 77-83); for more thorough treatments, see Theil (1967, Chapter 7) and Kloek (1966, Chapter 5), and for related material Rajaoja (1958, Chapter 3).

The restrictions linking price and income slopes are manifested again. Consider the form (2.2d) which uses q_y and Q_p^*. Engel aggregation appears again as

(2.15d) $p'q_y = 1$

as in (2.15a). Algebraically

$$\sum_i p_i \, (\partial q_i/\partial y) = 1.$$

For Cournot aggregation, postmultiply $Q_p^{*\prime}$ by p, obtaining

(2.16d) $Q_p^{*\prime}p = (Q_p + q_y \, q')'p = Q_p' \, p + q \, q_y' \, p = - q + q = 0$

in view of (2.16a) and (2.15d). Algebraically

$$\sum_i p_i \, (\partial q_i/\partial p_j)^* = 0 \qquad (j = 1, \ldots, n).$$

For symmetry,

(2.17d) $Q_p^{*\prime} = (Q_p + q_y \, q')' = Q_p + q_y \, q' = Q_p^*$

in view of (2.17a). Algebraically

$$(\partial q_i/\partial p_j)^* = (\partial q_j/\partial p_i)^* \qquad (i, j = 1, \ldots, n).$$

For homogeneity,

(2.18d) $Q_p^* \, p = (Q_p + q_y \, q')p = Q_p \, p + q_y \, q'p$

$$= - q_y \, y + q_y \, y = 0$$

in view of (2.18a) and $q'p = y$. Algebraically

$$\sum_j (\partial q_i/\partial p_j)^* \, p_j = 0 \qquad (i = 1, \ldots, n).$$

Another well-known result is that the utility-compensated own-price slope must be negative:

$$(\partial q_i/\partial p_i)^* < 0 \qquad (i = 1, \ldots, n);$$

for a concise proof, see Barten (1966, p. 22).

Now consider the form (2.2e) which uses q_y and Q_p^{**}. Once again Engel aggregation appears as

(2.15e)) $p'q_y = 1.$

Algebraically

$$\sum_i p_i (\partial q_i/\partial y) = 1.$$

For Cournot aggregation, postmultiply $Q_p^{**'}$ by p, obtaining

$$Q_p^{**'}p = (Q_p^* + \phi\ y\ q_y\ q_y')'p = Q_p^{*'}\ p + \phi\ y\ q_y\ q_y'\ p =$$

(2.16e) $$= \phi\ y\ q_y$$

in view of (2.16d) and (2.15e). Algebraically

$$\sum_i p_i (\partial q_i/\partial p_j)^{**} = \phi\ y\ (\partial q_j/\partial y) \quad (j = 1, \ldots, n).$$

Symmetry is apparent:

(2.17e) $$Q_p^{**'} = (Q_p^* + \phi\ y\ q_y\ q_y')' = Q_p^* + \phi\ y\ q_y\ q_y' = Q_p^{**}$$

in view of (2.17d). Algebraically

$$(\partial q_i/\partial p_j)^{**} = (\partial q_j/\partial p_i)^{**} \quad (i, j = 1, \ldots, n).$$

Homogeneity appears as

(2.18e) $$Q_p^{**}\ p = Q_p^{**'}\ p = \phi\ y\ q_y$$

in view of (2.17e) and (2.16e). Algebraically

$$\sum_j (\partial q_i/\partial p_j)^{**}\ p_j = \phi\ y\ (\partial q_i/\partial y) \quad (i = 1, \ldots, n).$$

Also, the marginal-utility-of-income-compensated own-price slope is negative:

$$(\partial q_i/\partial p_i)^{**} < 0 \qquad (i = 1, \ldots, n);$$

since $Q_p^{**} = \lambda\ U^{-1}$ is negative definite, its diagonal elements are negative.

These analyses of differentials and slopes may be translated into analyses of logarithmic differentials and elasticities. As in Section 2.1, we will work with the income elasticity vector

$$\eta = (\eta_1, \ldots, \eta_n)',$$

but we now introduce compensated price elasticity matrices

$$H^* = \begin{pmatrix} \eta^*_{11} & \cdots & \eta^*_{1n} \\ \vdots & & \vdots \\ \eta^*_{n1} & \cdots & \eta^*_{nn} \end{pmatrix}, \quad H^{**} = \begin{pmatrix} \eta^{**}_{11} & \cdots & \eta^{**}_{1n} \\ \vdots & & \vdots \\ \eta^{**}_{n1} & \cdots & \eta^{**}_{nn} \end{pmatrix}$$

where

$$\eta^*_{ij} = (\partial q_i/\partial p_j)^* \, (p_j/q_i), \qquad \eta^{**}_{ij} = (\partial q_i/\partial p_j)^{**} \, (p_j/q_i).$$

The matrix definitions of these in terms of Q^*_p and Q^{**}_p are clearly

$$H^* = \hat{q}^{-1} \, Q^*_p \, \hat{p} \quad , \qquad H^{**} = \hat{q}^{-1} \, Q^{**} \, \hat{p},$$

while in terms of H and η we may write

$$H^* = \hat{q}^{-1}(Q_p + q_y \, q') \, \hat{p} \quad , \qquad H^{**} = \hat{q}^{-1}(Q^*_p + \phi \, y \, q_y \, q'_y)\hat{p}$$

$$= H + \eta \, w' \qquad\qquad = H^* + \phi \, \eta \, w' \, \hat{\eta}$$

$$= H + \eta \, w' \, (I + \phi \, \hat{\eta}),$$

using $\eta = y \, \hat{q}^{-1} q_y$ and $w = y^{-1}\hat{p} \, q$.

A restatement of the demand functions and restrictions in terms of H^* or of H^{**} is straightforward. The logarithmic differential of the demand functions, originally expressed as

(2.2b) $\quad \text{dlog } q = \eta \text{ dlog } y + H \text{ dlog } p,$

may, in view of the definitions of H* and H**, alternatively be expressed as

(2.2f) $\quad \text{dlog } q = \eta \text{ (dlog } y - w' \text{ dlog } p) + H^* \text{ dlog } p,$

or as

(2.2g) $\text{dlog } q = \eta \text{ [dlog } y - w'(I + \phi \hat{\eta}) \text{ dlog } p] + H^{**} \text{ dlog } p$

$\qquad = \eta \text{ (dlog } y - w' \text{ dlog } p) + H^{**}(\text{dlog } p - \iota \, w' \hat{\eta} \text{ dlog } p)$

-- the last equality being based on the fact that $H^{**}\iota = \phi \eta$, as shown in (2.18g) below. While in (2.2b) η is the coefficient of the logchange in nominal income, in (2.2f) and (2.2g) it is the coefficient of the logchange in a deflated income variable. While in (2.2b) and (2.2f) the last term refers to logchanges in nominal prices, in (2.2g) it refers to logchanges in deflated prices. Stone (1953, p. 277) utilizes the formulation (2.2f); Barten (1964, p. 23) utilizes the formulation (2.2g).

The restrictions reappear as follows:

Engel aggregation:

(2.15f) $\quad w'\eta = 1$, $\qquad$ (2.15g) $\quad w'\eta = 1.$

Cournot aggregation:

(2.16f) $\quad H^{*\prime}w = (H+\eta w')'w$, $\qquad$ (2.16g) $\quad H^{**\prime}w = (H^*+\phi\eta w'\hat{\eta})'w$

$$= H'w + w\eta'w \qquad\qquad = H^{*\prime}w + \phi\hat{\eta}w\eta'w$$

$$= - w + w \qquad\qquad = \phi \, \hat{\eta} \, w$$

$$= 0 \qquad\qquad = \phi \, \hat{w} \, \eta.$$

Symmetry:

$$(2.17f)\quad (\hat{w}H^*)' = [\hat{w}(H+\eta w')]' = \hat{w}\,(H+\eta\, w') = \hat{w}\, H^*$$

$$(2.17g)\quad (\hat{w}H^{**})' = (\hat{w}H^*)' + (\phi\hat{w}\eta w'\hat{\eta})' = \hat{w}H^* + \phi\hat{w}\eta w'\hat{\eta} = \hat{w}\, H^{**}.$$

Homogeneity:

$$(2.18f)\quad H^*\iota = (H+\eta w')\iota = H\iota + \eta w'\iota = -\eta + \eta = 0$$

$$(2.18g)\quad H^{**}\iota = (H^*+\phi\eta w'\hat{\eta})\iota = H^*\iota + \phi\eta w'\eta = \phi\,\eta\, w'\eta = \phi\,\eta\,.$$

These analyses may be translated into terms of the budget share differentials. As in Section 2.1, we will work with the marginal budget share vector

$$\mu = (\mu_1, \ldots, \mu_n)',$$

but we now introduce compensated price response matrices

$$K = \begin{pmatrix} \kappa_{11} & \cdots & \kappa_{1n} \\ \vdots & & \vdots \\ \kappa_{n1} & \cdots & \kappa_{nn} \end{pmatrix} \qquad N = \begin{pmatrix} \nu_{11} & \cdots & \nu_{1n} \\ \vdots & & \vdots \\ \nu_{n1} & \cdots & \nu_{nn} \end{pmatrix}$$

defined by

$$K = y^{-1}\,\hat{p}\, Q_p^*\, \hat{p} = y^{-1}\,\hat{p}(Q_p + q_y\, q')\hat{p}$$

$$N = y^{-1}\hat{p}\, Q_p^{**}\, \hat{p} = y^{-1}\hat{p}(Q_p^* + \phi\, y\, q_y\, q_y')\hat{p}$$

$$= y^{-1}\hat{p}(Q_p + q_y\, q' + \phi\, y\, q_y\, q_y')\hat{p}$$

$$= \hat{w}\, H^* \qquad\qquad = \hat{w}\, H^{**}$$

$$= \hat{w}\, (H + \eta\, w') \qquad\qquad = \hat{w}\, (H^* + \phi\, \eta\, w'\hat{\eta})$$

$$= \hat{w}\, H + \mu\, w' \qquad\qquad = \hat{w}\, [H^* + \eta\, w'(I + \phi\, \hat{\eta})]$$

$$= \theta + \mu\, w' \qquad\qquad = \theta + \mu\, w'(I + \phi\, \hat{\eta})$$

$$= K + \phi\, \mu\, \mu'.$$

A restatement of the demand functions and restrictions in terms of K or of N is straightforward. The endogenous component of the budget share differential, originally expressed as

(2.2c) $\hat{w}\, d\log q = \mu\, d\log y + \theta\, d\log p,$

may, in view of the definitions of K and N, alternatively be expressed as

(2.2h) $\hat{w}\, d\log q = \mu\, (d\log y - w'\, d\log p) + K\, d\log p$

or as (2.2i):

$$\hat{w}\, d\log q = \mu\, (d\log y - (w + \phi\, \mu)'\, d\log p) + N\, d\log p$$

$$= \mu(d\log y - w'\, d\log p) + N(d\log p - \iota\, \mu'\, d\log p)$$

-- the last equality being based on the fact that $N\, \iota = \phi\, \mu$, as shown in (2.18i) below. The deflation is the same as that met in (2.2f) - (2.2g), for $w'\hat{\eta} = \mu'$. The formulation (2.2h) is used by Barten (1967) and by Parks (1969). It is, however, formulation (2.2i) which is featured in most recent work of the "Rotterdam School" (Parks' term); e.g., Barten (1966, Chapters 3-6) and Theil (1967, Chapter 7).

The restrictions now appear in elegant form:

Engel aggregation:

(2.15h) $\iota'\mu = 1$ (2.15i) $\iota'\mu = 1.$

Cournot aggregation:

(2.16h) $K'\iota = (\hat{w}\ H^*)'\iota$

$= H^{*\prime}w$

$= 0$

(2.16i) $N'\iota = (K + \phi\ \mu\ \mu')'\iota$

$= K'\iota + \phi\ \mu$

$= \phi\ \mu.$

Symmetry:

(2.17h) $K' = (\hat{w}\ H^*)'$

$= \hat{w}\ H^*$

$= K$

(2.17i) $N' = (K + \phi\ \mu\ \mu')'$

$= K' + \phi\ \mu\ \mu'$

$= K + \phi\ \mu\ \mu'$

$= N.$

Homogeneity:

(2.18h) $K\iota = K'\iota$

$= 0$

(2.18i) $N\iota = N'\iota$

$= \phi\ \mu.$

Finally, we note that

(2.21) $\iota'\ N\ \iota = \phi;$

a fact which may be obtained by premultiplication of (2.18i) by ι' since $\iota'\mu = 1$; or to return to fundamentals, from

$$N = y^{-1}\ \hat{p}\ Q_p^{**}\ \hat{p} = \lambda\ y^{-1}\ \hat{p}\ U^{-1}\ \hat{p},$$

which implies

$$\iota' N \iota = \lambda\ y^{-1}\ p' U^{-1} p = \lambda\ y^{-1}\ \lambda_y^{-1} = \phi,$$

since $\lambda_y = (p' U^{-1} p)^{-1}$.

We should now pause and take stock of the alternative representations of the differentials of the demand functions which have been developed. The following scheme may help to keep the basic structure in mind.

	Dependent Variable		
	dq	$d\log q$	$\hat{w}\, d\log q$
Price change:			
Uncompensated	Q_p	H	θ
Utility-compensated	$Q_p^* = Q_p + q_y q'$	$H^* = H + \eta w'$	$K = \theta + \mu w'$
Marginal-utility compensated	$Q^{**} = Q^* + \phi y q_y q'$ $= \lambda\, U^{-1}$	$H^{**} = H^* + \phi \eta w' \hat{\eta}$ $= \lambda \hat{q}^{-1} U^{-1} \hat{p}$	$N = K + \phi\, \mu\mu'$ $= \lambda y^{-1} \hat{p} U^{-1} \hat{p}$
Income change:	q_y	$\eta = y\, \hat{q}^{-1} q_y$	$\mu = \hat{p}\, q_y = \hat{w}\eta$

For each of the nine formulations (2.2a)-(2.2i), equations linking the price and income slopes within and across demand functions have been established.

Under any of the representations being considered here, the force of the classical theory is to reduce the number of free "coefficients" in a complete set of demand functions. The reduction arises as a consequence of the restrictions which link the price and income coefficients in any set of demand functions which has been generated by a classical utility maximization process. These economies of parameterization are not costless, of course. All dynamic considerations are being ignored, as are possible feedbacks from demand to prices and income. In drawing on this theory for the analysis of national data, we may be sacrificing intelligence for elegance when we presume that the consumer sector behaves as if it were maximizing a collective utility function.

2.3 Additive Utility

We turn to specializations of the foregoing results which obtain in the special case where the direct utility function u = u(q) is additive, that is when

(2.22) $$u = u(q_1, \ldots, q_n) = \sum_{i=1}^{n} u^i(q_i),$$

each $u^i(\ )$ being a function of only the corresponding q_i. We refer to this feature as direct additivity; alternative verbalizations include "want-independence," "complete want-independence," "preference independence." As Frisch (1959) and Houthakker (1960a) have demonstrated, direct additivity has important implications for the complete set of demand functions. We trace these implications through the alternative representations of the demand functions developed in Sections 2.1-2.2, in reverse order.

The key is the diagonality of the second derivative matrix U. If u(q) is directly additive, then the marginal utility of any good varies with the quantity of that good alone, so $u_{ij} = 0$ ($i \neq j$; $i,j = 1,\ldots,n$); thus U is diagonal.

Then U^{-1} is also diagonal; specifically

$$u^{ij} = \begin{cases} u_{ii}^{-1} & \text{if } i = j \\ 0 & \text{if } i \neq j\ . \end{cases}$$

Now, regardless of additivity, we have seen that

$$N = \lambda\, y^{-1}\hat{p}\, U^{-1}\hat{p}.$$

Algebraically

$$\nu_{ij} = \lambda\, y^{-1} p_i p_j u^{ij}.$$

Under direct additivity, therefore

$$\nu_{ij} = \begin{cases} \lambda\, y^{-1} p_i^2\, u_{ii}^{-1} & \text{if } i = j \\ 0 & \text{if } i \neq j \end{cases} ,$$

that is, N is diagonal. Since regardless of additivity $N\iota = \phi\,\mu$, under direct additivity we have

$$N = \phi\,\hat{\mu}.$$

Algebraically

$$\nu_{ij} = \begin{cases} \phi\,\mu_i & \text{if } i = j \\ 0 & \text{if } i \neq j\,. \end{cases}$$

Then since $K = N - \phi\,\mu\,\mu'$ in any case, under direct additivity we have

$$K = \phi\,\hat{\mu} - \phi\,\mu\,\mu' = \phi\,(\hat{\mu} - \mu\,\mu') = \phi\,\hat{\mu}\,(I - \iota\,\mu').$$

Algebraically

$$\kappa_{ij} = \begin{cases} \phi\,\mu_i(1 - \mu_i) & \text{if } i = j \\ -\,\phi\,\mu_i\,\mu_j & \text{if } i \neq j. \end{cases}$$

Proceeding, since $H^{**} = \hat{w}^{-1}N$ in any case, under direct additivity we have

$$H^{**} = \hat{w}^{-1}(\phi\,\hat{\mu}) = \phi\,\hat{w}^{-1}\hat{w}\,\hat{\eta} = \phi\,\hat{\eta}\,.$$

Algebraically

$$\eta^{**}_{ij} = \begin{cases} \phi\,\eta_i & \text{if } i = j \\ 0 & \text{if } i \neq j. \end{cases}$$

Since $H^{*} = H^{**} - \phi\,\eta\,w'\hat{\eta}$ in any case, under direct additivity we have

$$H^{*} = \phi\,\hat{\eta} - \phi\,\eta\,w'\,\hat{\eta} = \phi\,\hat{\eta}(I - \iota\,w'\,\hat{\eta}).$$

Algebraically

$$\eta^{*}_{ij} = \begin{cases} \phi\,\eta_i\,(1 - w_i\eta_i) & \text{if } i = j \\ -\phi\,\eta_i\eta_j\,w_j & \text{if } i \neq j. \end{cases}$$

Since $Q_p^{**} = \hat{q}\ H^{**}\ \hat{p}^{-1}$ in any case, under direct additivity we have

$$Q_p^{**} = \hat{q}\ \phi\ \hat{\eta}\ \hat{p}^{-1} = \phi\ y\ \hat{p}^{-1}\hat{q}_y.$$

Algebraically

$$(\partial q_i/\partial p_j)^{**} = \begin{cases} \phi\ y\ p_i^{-1}(\partial q_i/\partial y) & \text{if } i = j \\ 0 & \text{if } i \neq j. \end{cases}$$

Since $Q_p^{*} = Q_p^{**} - \phi\ y\ q_y\ q_y'$ in any case, under direct additivity we have

$$Q_p^{*} = \phi\ y\ \hat{p}^{-1}\hat{q}_y - \phi\ y\ q_y\ q_y' = \phi\ y\ (\hat{p}^{-1}\hat{q}_y - q_y\ q_y')$$

$$= \phi\ y\ \hat{q}_y\ (\hat{p}^{-1} - \iota\ q_y').$$

Algebraically

$$(\partial q_i/\partial p_j)^{*} = \begin{cases} \phi\ y\ (\partial q_i/\partial y)[p_i^{-1} - (\partial q_i/\partial y)] & \text{if } i = j \\ -\ \phi\ y\ (\partial q_i/\partial y)(\partial q_j/\partial y) & \text{if } i \neq j \end{cases}$$

which are equations (11) and (13) in Houthakker (1960a, p. 248).

Since $\Theta = K - \mu\ w'$ in any case, under direct additivity we have

$$\Theta = \phi\ (\hat{\mu} - \mu\ \mu') - \mu\ w' = \phi\ \hat{\mu} - \mu\ (w + \phi\ \mu)'.$$

Algebraically

$$\theta_{ij} = \begin{cases} \phi\ \mu_i - \mu_i\ (w_i + \phi\ \mu_i) & \text{if } i = j \\ -\ \mu_i\ (w_j + \phi\ \mu_j) & \text{if } i \neq j. \end{cases}$$

Since $H = H^* - \eta\, w'$ in any case, under direct additivity we have

$$H = \phi\, \hat{\eta}\, (I - \iota\, w'\hat{\eta}) - \eta\, w' = \phi\, \hat{\eta} - \eta\, w'(I + \phi\, \hat{\eta}).$$

Algebraically

$$\eta_{ij} = \begin{cases} \phi\, \eta_i - \eta_i\, w_i(1 + \phi\, \eta_i) & \text{if } i = j \\ - \eta_i\, w_j(1 + \phi\, \eta_j) & \text{if } i \neq j \end{cases}$$

which is comparable to equations (61) and (62) in Frisch (1959, pp. 186-187). Finally, since $Q_p = Q_p^* - q_y\, q'$ in any case, under direct additivity we have

$$Q_p = \phi\, y\, \hat{q}_y\, (\hat{p}^{-1} - \iota\, q_y') - q_y\, q'$$

$$= \phi\, y\, \hat{q}_y\, \hat{p}^{-1} - q_y(q + \phi\, y\, q_y)'.$$

Algebraically

$$(\partial q_i/\partial p_j) = \begin{cases} \phi y(\partial q_i/\partial y)p_i^{-1} - (\partial q_i/\partial y)[q_i + \phi y(\partial q_i/\partial y)] \\ \qquad \text{if } i = j \\ - (\partial q_i/\partial y)\, [q_j + \phi\, y\, (\partial q_j/\partial y)] \\ \qquad \text{if } i \neq j. \end{cases}$$

In summary, under any of the representations, the force of the additivity assumption is to reduce the number of free "coefficients." The price slope matrices Q_p, Q_p^*, and Q_p^{**} are expressible in terms of the income slope vector q_y and the scalar income flexibility ϕ. The price elasticity matrices H, H*, and H** are expressible in terms of the income elasticity vector η and ϕ. The price response matrices Θ, K, and N are expressible in terms of the marginal budget share vector μ and ϕ. (The observables y, p, q, and w are taken for granted in these statements.) Thus a directly-additive utility function would lead to substantial economies in parameterizing a complete set of demand functions, beyond those obtained from the general utility function of Sections 2.1 and 2.2.

Nor are these economies costless. As noted by Houthakker (1960a, p. 248), direct additivity rules out the possibility of specific substitution effects: with all $u^{ij} = 0$ for $i \neq j$, all ν_{ij}, η^{**}_{ij}, and $(\partial q_i/\partial p_j)^{**}$ are zero for $i \neq j$. As noted by Theil (1967, p. 199), direct additivity rules out inferior goods: with $\mu_i = \nu_{ii}/\phi$, $\nu_{ii} < 0$, and $\phi < 0$, all μ_i must be positive, and thus all η_i and $(\partial q_i/\partial y)$ are positive. Further, direct additivity rules out the possibility of complementary goods: with $\kappa_{ij} = -\phi\, \mu_i \mu_j$ $(i \neq j)$, $\phi < 0$, $\mu_i > 0$, and $\mu_j > 0$, all κ_{ij} must be positive for $i \neq j$ and thus all η^*_{ij} and $(\partial q_i/\partial p_j)^*$ are positive for $i \neq j$. In the light of these restrictions, direct additivity may be a plausible specification when goods are defined broadly, but not when one works with a fine classification of consumer expenditures. In the latter case, specific substitution effects, complementarities, and inferiorities may well be present.

2.4 Monotonic Transformations of the Utility Function

We have been using a cardinal utility function, so that the question arises as to which of our results hold up under monotonic transformations of the utility function. In an environment of certainty, observable changes in quantities demanded in response to changes in income and prices will not permit one to identify a particular utility function out of a set of its monotonic transforms. All members of the set describe the same underlying preference ordering; their indifference map is the same apart from relabelling.

Let $v = v(u) = v(u(q)) = \tilde{v}(q)$ be a monotonically increasing function of u, that is $v_u = dv/du > 0$. For given y and p the maximum of v subject to $p'q = y$ is attained at the same q that maximizes u subject to $p'q = y$. That is to say, the set of demand functions $q = q(y,p)$ is invariant with respect to monotonic transformations of the utility function; this is the very source of the lack of identifiability. With the demand functions invariant, the slopes q_y and Q_p are certainly invariant; thus the elasticities η and H and the responses μ and θ are also. With all three terms on the right of

$$Q_p^* = Q_p + q_y q'$$

invariant, the left-hand side must also be. Thus Q_p^* and hence H* and K are invariant with respect to monotonic transformations of the utility function. That is to say, Slutsky's decomposition of the response to a price change into an income and a substitution effect holds up under monotonic transformations of the utility function. A related point is that the income needed to maintain v in the face of a price change is the same as the income needed to maintain u in the face of the same price change. Thus the utility-maintaining income compensation $(dy)^* = q'dp$ is the same under v as under u. Indeed, in the large as well as in the small, the true cost of living index (defined as 1 plus the proportionate change in income required to maintain utility) is invariant.

Other features of the theory, however, are not invariant. Clearly the new indirect function

$$v = \tilde{v}(q(y,p)) = v^*(y, p) = v(u^*(y, p))$$

will differ from $u^*(y, p)$ unless $v(u)$ is the identity transformation; similarly the new marginal utility of income function $\mu = \partial v/\partial y = \mu(y, p)$ will differ from $\lambda = \lambda(y, p)$ unless $v(u)$ is u plus a constant.

To be more specific we may proceed as follows. Let v_q denote the n x 1 marginal utility vector under v. Then

$$v_q = \partial v/\partial q = (dv/du)(\partial u/\partial q) = v_u u_q$$

will differ from the marginal utility vector under u, u_q, unless $v_u = 1$, in which case $v = u + \text{constant}$. The marginal rates of transformation between goods -- i.e., the ratios of elements of the marginal utility vector -- are invariant since v_q is a scalar multiple of u_q. Let V denote the n x n second derivative matrix under v. Then

$$V = \partial^2 v/\partial q \partial q' = \partial v_q/\partial q' = \partial(v_u u_q)/\partial q'$$

$$= v_u\ (\partial u_q/\partial q') + u_q\ v_{uu}\ (\partial u/\partial q')$$

$$(2.23) \qquad = v_u\ U + v_{uu}\ u_q\ u_q'$$

will in general differ from U unless $v_u = 1$ (and $v_{uu} = 0$) in which case v = u + constant. Let κ denote the marginal utility of income under v. Then

$$\kappa = \partial v/\partial y = (dv/du)(\partial u/\partial y) = v_u\ \lambda$$

will differ from λ unless again $v_u = 1$. Let κ_y denote the income slope of the marginal utility of income. Then

$$\kappa_y = \partial\kappa/\partial y = \partial(v_u\lambda)/\partial y = v_u(\partial\lambda/\partial y) + \lambda\ (\partial v_u/\partial y)$$

$$= v_u\ \lambda_y + \lambda^2\ v_{uu}$$

will in general differ from λ_y unless again $v_u = 1$ (and $v_{uu} = 0$). Let $\eta_{\kappa y}$ denote the income elasticity of the marginal utility of income under v. Then

$$\eta_{\kappa y} = \kappa_y\ y\ \kappa^{-1} = (v_u\ \lambda_y + \lambda^2\ v_{uu})\ y\ (v_u\ \lambda)^{-1}$$

$$= \lambda_y\ y\ \lambda^{-1} + \lambda\ y\ v_{uu}\ v_u^{-1}$$

$$= \eta_{\lambda y} + \lambda\ y\ v_{uu}\ v_u^{-1}$$

will differ from $\eta_{\lambda y}$ unless $v_{uu} = 0$, in which case v is a linear function of u. Similarly the income flexibility under v, $\eta_{\kappa y}^{-1}$, will differ from the income flexibility under u, $\phi = \eta_{\lambda y}^{-1}$, unless v is a linear function of u.

Leaving linear transformations aside, we see that monotonic transformations of the utility function, while not affecting the Slutsky decomposition of the response to a price change into an income and substitution effect, do affect the further (Frisch-Houthakker) decomposition of the substitution effect into a general and specific component. Since $N = K + \phi \mu \mu'$, the invariance of K and μ makes N variable with ϕ; N and hence H** and Q_p^{**} are not invariant. To see this for Q_p^{**} directly: we know that under u, $Q_p^{**} = \lambda U^{-1}$, that is $(Q_p^{**})^{-1} = \lambda^{-1}U$. The corresponding compensated price slope matrix inverse under v would be

$$\kappa^{-1}V = (v_u\lambda)^{-1}(v_u U + v_{uu} u_q u_q')$$
$$= \lambda^{-1}U + v_{uu} (v_u\lambda)^{-1}u_q u_q' ,$$

which differs from $\lambda^{-1}U$ unless $v_{uu} = 0$. A related point is that the income needed to maintain κ in the face of a price change will in general differ from the income needed to maintain λ in the face of the same price change. Thus the marginal-utility-of-income maintaining income compensation (dy)** [= $(\phi\ y\ q_y + q)'dp$ under u] is in general not invariant under monotonic transformations of the utility function.

It is also apparent that direct additivity is not an invariant under monotonic transformations. For suppose that U is diagonal; then

$$V = v_u U + v_{uu} u_q u_q'$$

will in general not be diagonal unless $v_{uu} = 0$, that is unless v is a linear function of u. Consequently "want-independence" is not an invariant across nonlinear transformations. Does this suggest that the restrictions on the demand functions which are based on an assumption of direct additivity are meaningless? By no means. For if "want-independence" is not invariant, then neither is "want-dependence"; a given preference ordering may have a directly-additive representation. Given a non-additive utility function, it may be possible to find a monotonic transform of it which is directly additive.[4] If this is so then it is clearly advantageous to represent the ordering by the additive utility function, to exploit the economy of parameterization. The restrictions which flow from the additivity assumption are operational: if the true utility function belongs to a set of monotonic transforms which has an additive member, then the demand behavior which results from maximizing it will satisfy the restrictions which flow from additivity.[5]

A final point, whose full implications will not be examined here, is that the negative definiteness of the second derivative matrix is not an invariant under nonlinear transformations: even if U is nonsingular, $v_u^{-1} V = U + v_{uu} v^{-1} u_q u_q'$ need not be.

2.5 Welfare Indicators

We have introduced the utility function as an aid to positive economics, that is, as a guide to the specification of complete sets of consumer demand functions. It is tempting to consider its implications for normative economics, that is, its use as a guide to the construction of welfare indicators. Because our empirical material deals with international data this temptation is particularly strong. Any such normative use will, of course, proceed on the assumption that the utility function is the same in all situations being compared.

A comparison of welfare across two income-price situations should in principle be based on the computation of the (maximum attainable) utility in the two situations. That is to say, the indirect utility function $u^*(y, p)$ would itself serve as a welfare indicator. A variant of this takes real income as the welfare indicator: The true cost of living index, constructed with one situation taken as the reference base, is used to deflate nominal income in the second situation, yielding a real income measure which is directly comparable with income in the reference situation. This amounts to employing a monotonic transformation of the indirect utility function, $v = v(u)$, in which $v^*(y^o, p^o) = y^o$ and $v^*(y^1, p^1) = y^1/(y^*/y^o)$ where the superscripts o and 1 denote the reference and second situations respectively, and (y^*/y^o) is the true cost of living index.

In actuality the utility function will be unknown so that the "ideal" method just sketched is unavailable. An established procedure is to develop a more or less sophisticated approximation to the true cost of living index which is then used to deflate nominal income, yielding an approximation to real income. Data requirements, complexities, and ambiguities are often substantial.

Running counter to this established procedure is an underground tradition which seeks to bypass the details of the price structure in favor of some summary indicator of the consumer's situation. One stream looks to the composition of expenditures. For example, the proportion of income spent on food is taken as an (inverse) indicator of welfare, the presumption being that this average budget share surely falls as real income rises. This particular indicator enjoys widespread informal use. The "iso-prop index" developed by Watts (1967) for adjusting a national poverty standard to varying consumer conditions, represents a sophisticated extension of this device.

Another stream, whose chief navigator has been Frisch, looks to the marginal utility of income function $\lambda = \lambda(y, p)$ as a basis for comparing welfare. Specifically, Frisch (1932) proposed that the "money flexibility" -- in our terminology the income elasticity of the marginal utility of income, $\eta_{\lambda y}$ -- serves as an indicator of welfare. (Equivalently, the income flexibility, $\phi = \eta_{\lambda y}^{-1}$, serves as an inverse indicator of welfare.) Here the presumption appears to be that the marginal utility of income λ is very high at low income levels and approaches zero at high income levels. If this is so, then $\eta_{\lambda y}$ will move from large negative values at low income levels to small negative values at high income levels, thus serving as an indicator of welfare

To get the flavor of this approach, it is worth citing a passage from Chapter 9 of Frisch (1932). In the earlier chapters of this monograph, Frisch worked out several procedures for estimating the "money flexibility function" ($\eta_{\lambda y}$ as a function of income). In Chapter 9, which is entitled "Money utility and the problem of index numbers," he first develops the argument that a "price of living index" (= true cost of living index) is a device for "reducing" (= converting) incomes in different situations into comparable units. The basic complication -- lucidly re-exposited in Frisch (1954) -- is that such an index should be a function rather than a single number. He then develops the argument that the money flexibility function may be used for converting incomes:

I now proceed to the more general aspect of the connection between the notion of money utility and the problem of index numbers. The main idea back of our attempt to construct an index number of "the price of living" is, I think, this: We have two points of time (or place), Nos. (1) and (2). And we want to know by how much we must multiply the income in (1) in order to get an income in (2) that will make an individual just as well off ... Let ρ_1 be a given nominal income in the first point of time (or place), and ρ_2 the corresponding nominal income in the second point of time (or place), i.e. the income that would make the individual just as well off as he is with the income ρ_1 in the first point of time (or place). In the orthodox formulation of the index number problem it is implicitly assumed that the income ρ_2 in question can be found simply by multiplying ρ_1 by a certain factor P_{21} which is independent of ρ_1 ... And this constant P_{21} is just taken as an expression for the "living price" at the point of time (or place) No. (2) as compared with the "living price" at the point of time (or place) No. (1). It seems to me that the whole index number problem appears in a more fruitful setting when we drop the orthodox assumption that P_{21} is a constant, and simply formulate the notion of "living price" by saying that ρ_2 is some function of ρ_1

$$\rho_2 = R_{21}(\rho_1).$$

... The curve that gives a graphical picture of the function R_{21} ... we shall call the reduction curve between the two points considered. It expresses the rule by which ρ_2 is reduced to a scale where it becomes comparable with ρ_1 ...
Is it to be expected that the "living price" ratio between, say Berlin and Rome should be exactly the same when it is defined by a comparison between workmens wages as when it is defined by a comparison between salaries for ambassadors? Certainly not ...
In terms of the notions here developed the problem of living price determination is the problem of defining some principle by which, to every income ρ_1 in (1) we can associate a certain income ρ_2 in (2). If the mode of living is not very much alike in the two situations, it appears as exceedingly difficult to

make this association on the basis of direct observation of prices and quantities. This is true already in the simple case when P_{21} is assumed constant, and it would be still more true in the case where we consider P_{21} as a function of ρ_1. In particular it seems that these difficulties would be virtually insurmountable when the comparisons made are geographical rather than temporal.
The question therefore arises: Does there exist any economic parameter which is a pure number, defined only by prices and quantities in (1) or only by prices and quantities in (2) (so that no direct price comparison between (1) and (2) is necessary), and which further is such that it offers a possibility of creating a plausible association between ρ_1 and ρ_2? ...
It seems more or less inevitable to attach the real income definition to some basic feature of human behavior which we know depends very closely upon how high up in the scale of living the individual finds himself ... And a quantitative measure of this behavior is just the money flexibility.
The practical carrying through of this principle would be as follows: Let us assume that the money flexibility functions $\tilde{w}_1(\rho_1)$ and $\tilde{w}_2(\rho_2)$ for (1) and (2) are determined by some method or another. And let us assume that both these functions are monotonic functions, so that a given $\tilde{w}_1$ will determine uniquely a certain ρ_1, and a given $\tilde{w}_2$ will determine uniquely a certain ρ_2. If this is so, we can determine an association between ρ_1 and ρ_2 by the following process. First select a certain magnitude of ρ_1. Then determine what flexibility $\tilde{w}_1$ in (1) corresponds to this ρ_1. Then go to that point on the flexibility curve for (2) where the flexibility is equal to $\tilde{w}_1$. And finally read off what income ρ_2 in (2) corresponds to this flexibility ... By virtue of our assumption regarding the monotony of the two functions ... [this] will define ρ_2 uniquely as a function of ρ_1.

Frisch (1932, pp. 74-79).

Returning to positive economics, we have seen that $\eta_{\lambda y}$ (actually its reciprocal ϕ) appears as a key "parameter" in the analysis of complete sets of demand functions. This role is particularly striking under direct additivity for then a knowledge of ϕ enables one to compute all price coefficients from the income coefficients. This raises the possibility of estimating price elasticities from cross-section samples even though no price variation is observed. This possibility is explored in Frisch (1959), an article which contains the now-famous passage:

> We may perhaps, assume that in most cases the money flexibility has values of the order of magnitude given below.
>
> $\tilde{w}$ {
> -10 for an extremely poor and apathetic part of the population.
> - 4 for the slightly better off but still poor part of the population with a fairly pronounced desire to become better off.
> - 2 for the middle income bracket, "the median part" of the population.
> - 0.7 for the better-off part of the population.
> - 0.1 for the rich part of the population with ambitions towards "conspicuous consumption".
>
> It would be a very promising research project to determine $\tilde{w}$ for different countries and for different types of populations. A universal "atlas" of the values of $\tilde{w}$ should be constructed. It would serve an extremely useful purpose in demand analysis.
>
> Frisch (1959, p. 189).

This suggestion has been taken up by later authors. Thus Barten (1964, p. 22), Powell (1965, p. 565), Powell (1966, p. 674), and Powell et al. (1968) have reported (for Holland, Canada, Australia, and the U.S.A. respectively) values of $\eta_{\lambda y}$ in the range -1.5 to -2.5, based on aggregate time series data.

Even if our concern is strictly with positive economics, therefore, it will be of interest to consider $\eta_{\lambda y}$ in the context of a complete set of consumer demand functions. If this measure is to serve as a welfare indicator, however, it is essential that it be monotonic -- presumably increasing algebraically -- in real income. We have seen that the value of $\eta_{\lambda y}$ is not invariant under nonlinear transformations of the utility function, so that its monotonicity may not be invariant.[6] Frisch himself (1959, p. 184, n. 5) remarks "Whether it is realistic to assume that the money flexibility $\tilde{\omega}$ [i.e. $\eta_{\lambda y}$] is approximately a function of the indifference level, is another question."[7] The direction of the relation between $\eta_{\lambda y}$ and y turns out to involve the third derivative of the indirect utility function, $\partial^3 u^*/\partial y^3 = \partial^2\lambda/\partial y^2 = \partial\lambda_y/\partial y = \lambda_{yy}$, say. For,

$$\partial\eta_{\lambda y}/\partial y = \partial(\lambda_y \lambda^{-1} y)/\partial y = \lambda_y \lambda^{-1} - \lambda_y \lambda^{-2} \lambda_y y + \lambda_{yy} \lambda^{-1} y$$

$$= \eta_{\lambda y} y^{-1}[1 - \eta_{\lambda y} + \lambda_{yy} \lambda_y^{-1} y].$$

With $\eta_{\lambda y} < 0$ the term outside the brackets is negative, while inside the brackets $1 - \eta_{\lambda y} > 0$ and $\lambda_y^{-1} y < 0$; thus

a <u>necessary</u> condition for $\eta_{\lambda y}$ to rise with income is that λ_{yy} be positive. Other than this, we have been unable to characterize the class of utility functions for which $\eta_{\lambda y}$ rises with income as Frisch's basic argument would seem to require.

3

LINEAR EXPENDITURE SYSTEM

3.1 Derivation of Complete Set of Demand Functions

We now turn to consider the model of consumer demand which results when the utility function is of the Stone-Geary form

$$u = \sum_{i=1}^{n} \beta_i \log (q_i - \gamma_i),$$

in which the β's and γ's are parameters with

$$0 < \beta_i < 1 , \qquad 0 \leqslant \gamma_i \qquad (i = 1,\ldots,n)$$

$$\sum_{i=1}^{n} \beta_i = 1,$$

the function being defined only for

$$0 < (q_i - \gamma_i) \qquad (i = 1,\ldots,n).$$

This function was shown by Geary (1949) to justify a true cost of living index which had been proposed by Klein and Rubin (1947). The demand functions which it generates have been developed and applied extensively by Stone (1954, 1962, 1964, 1965, 1966) and Stone, Brown, and Rowe (1964).

Defining the parameter vectors

$$\beta = (\beta_1,\ldots,\beta_n)', \qquad \gamma = (\gamma_1,\ldots,\gamma_n)' ,$$

we may express the function as

$$(3.1) \quad u = \beta' \log (q - \gamma) ,$$

$$0 < \beta < \iota, \quad 0 \leqslant \gamma, \quad \iota'\beta = 1, \quad 0 < (q - \gamma).$$ [8]

Differentiating u with respect to q gives the vector of marginal utilities of the goods

$$u_q = \partial u/\partial q = (\hat{q} - \hat{\gamma})^{-1}\beta .$$

Algebraically

$$u_i = \partial u/\partial q_i = \beta_i(q_i - \gamma_i)^{-1} \quad (i = 1,\ldots,n).$$

With $\beta > 0$ and $(q - \gamma) > 0$, clearly $u_q > 0$. The second derivative matrix is

$$U = \partial u_q/\partial q' = -(\hat{q} - \hat{\gamma})^{-1}\hat{\beta}(\hat{q} - \hat{\gamma})^{-1}.$$

Algebraically

$$u_{ij} = \partial^2 u/\partial q_i \partial q_j = \begin{cases} -\beta_i(q_i - \gamma_i)^{-2} & \text{if } i = j \\ 0 & \text{if } i \neq j \end{cases}$$

$$(i,j = 1,\ldots,n).$$

The Stone-Geary utility function is thus directly additive. With $\beta_i > 0$ and $(q_i - \gamma_i) > 0$ for all i, diminishing marginal utility prevails for each good. The matrix U is diagonal and has all its diagonal elements negative; thus it is negative definite. Its inverse

$$U^{-1} = -(\hat{q} - \hat{\gamma})\hat{\beta}^{-1}(\hat{q} - \hat{\gamma})$$

is similarly negative definite.

The complete set of demand functions which results from maximizing u subject to $p'q = y$, with y and p given, may be found as follows. Setting $u_q = \lambda\, p$ gives

$$(\hat{q} - \hat{\gamma})^{-1}\beta \quad = \lambda\, p,$$

that is

$$(3.2) \qquad \beta \; = \lambda\, (\hat{q} - \hat{\gamma})\; p = \lambda\, \hat{p}\; (q - \gamma).$$

Premultiplying by ι' and using $\iota'\beta = 1$ and $p'q = y$ yields

$$1 = \iota'\beta = \lambda\; \iota'\hat{p}(q - \gamma) = \lambda\; p'(q - \gamma) = \lambda(y - p'\gamma)$$

whence

$$(3.3) \qquad \lambda = (y - p'\gamma)^{-1}.$$

Algebraically

$$\lambda = (y - \textstyle\sum_i p_i\gamma_i)^{-1}.$$

Inserting (3.3) into (3.2) gives

$$\beta = (y - p'\gamma)^{-1}\hat{p}\; (q - \gamma)$$

whence

$$\hat{p}(q - \gamma) = (y - p'\gamma)\beta,$$

or

$$(3.4) \qquad \hat{p}\; q = \hat{p}\; \gamma + (y - p'\gamma)\; \beta;$$

finally

$$(3.5) \qquad q = \gamma + (y - p'\gamma)\; \hat{p}^{-1}\; \beta.$$

Algebraically, the last two equations read

$$p_i q_i = p_i\gamma_i + \beta_i(y - \textstyle\sum_j p_j\gamma_j) \qquad (i = 1,\ldots,n)$$

$$q_i = \gamma_i + \beta_i p_i^{-1}(y - \textstyle\sum_j p_j\gamma_j) \qquad (i = 1,\ldots,n).$$

Equation (3.4) may be written as

$$\hat{p}\, q = y\, \beta + \hat{p}\, \gamma - p'\gamma\, \beta$$

$$= y\, \beta + \hat{\gamma}\, p - \beta\, \gamma' p$$

$$= y\, \beta + (I - \beta\, \iota')\, \hat{\gamma}\, p. \tag{3.6}$$

Algebraically

$$p_i q_i = \beta_i\, y + \sum_{j=1}^{n} (\delta_{ij} - \beta_i)\gamma_j p_j \quad (i = 1,\ldots,n)$$

where

$$\delta_{ij} = \begin{cases} 1 & \text{if } i = j \\ 0 & \text{if } i \neq j \end{cases}$$

is the Kronecker delta. Thus in the present model expenditure on each good is a (homogeneous) linear function of income and all prices. For this reason the model is referred to as the <u>linear expenditure system</u>, or more precisely as Stone's linear expenditure system.

A useful interpretation of the parameters of this system is available. Given income y and prices $p_1,\ldots,p_n$, the consumer first purchases "minimum required quantities" of each good: γ_1 of good $1,\ldots,\gamma_n$ of good n. At the given prices, this costs $\sum_j p_j \gamma_j$, which may be termed "subsistence income." He is left with $y-\sum_j p_j q_j$, which may be termed "supernumerary income"; this he distributes among the goods in the proportions $\beta_1,\ldots,\beta_n$. (The β's are thus identified with the μ's, the marginal budget shares, of Section 2.2.) Recall that the utility function is defined only for $(q_i - \gamma_i) > 0$ $(i = 1,\ldots,n)$; it makes no prediction about the behavior of a consumer for whom $y - \sum_j p_j \gamma_j = \sum_j p_j (q_j - \gamma_j) < 0$ since he cannot afford to acquire $\gamma_1,\ldots,\gamma_n$ at the going prices. There is of course no need to interpret the γ's as physical minima.[9]

Now consider the demand functions themselves. The income slope vector is readily found from (3.5):

$$q_y = \partial q/\partial y = \hat{p}^{-1}\beta. \tag{3.7}$$

Algebraically

$$(\partial q_i/\partial y) = \beta_i p_i^{-1} \qquad (i = 1,\ldots,n).$$

The Engel curves which relate quantities to income, all prices being given, are linear:

$$q_i = (\gamma_i - \beta_i p_i^{-1} \sum_j p_j \gamma_j) + (\beta_i p_i^{-1}) y \quad (i = 1, \ldots, n),$$

the linearity being already apparent from the fact that $(\partial q_i/\partial y)$ does not vary with y. The price slope matrix is also readily found:

$$(3.8) \qquad Q_p = \partial q/\partial p' = - (y - p'\gamma)\, \hat{p}^{-1}\, \hat{\beta}\, \hat{p}^{-1} - \hat{p}^{-1} \beta\, \gamma'.$$

Algebraically

$$(\partial q_i/\partial p_j) = \begin{cases} -(y - p'\gamma)\beta_i p_i^{-2} - \beta_i \gamma_i p_i^{-1} & \text{if } i = j \\ \qquad\qquad\qquad\quad - \beta_i \gamma_j p_i^{-1} & \text{if } i \neq j. \end{cases}$$

The "textbook" demand curves which relate quantities to own-prices, income and all other prices being given, are hyperbolic:

$$q_i = [(1 - \beta_i)\gamma_i] + [\beta_i (y - \sum_{j \neq i} p_j \gamma_j)] p_i^{-1} \quad ,$$

the hyperbolicity being already apparent from the form of $(\partial q_i/\partial p_i)$.[10]

It is not hard to see that q_y and Q_p satisfy the restrictions (2.15a) - (2.18a), as indeed they must since the linear expenditure system has been obtained by classical utility maximization. Thus

$$p'q_y = p'\hat{p}^{-1}\beta = \iota'\beta = 1;$$

$$\begin{aligned} Q_p' \, p &= - (y - p'\gamma)\, \hat{p}^{-1}\, \hat{\beta}\, \hat{p}^{-1} p - \gamma\, \beta'\hat{p}^{-1} p \\ &= - (y - p'\gamma)\, \hat{p}^{-1}\, \hat{\beta}\, \iota \qquad - \gamma\, \beta'\iota \\ &= - [(y - p'\gamma)\, \hat{p}^{-1}\beta + \gamma] \\ &= - q; \end{aligned}$$

$$(Q_p + q_y q')' = -[(y-p'\gamma)\hat{p}^{-1}\hat{\beta} + \gamma\beta']\hat{p}^{-1} + [\gamma + (y-p'\gamma)\hat{p}^{-1}\beta]\beta'\hat{p}^{-1}$$

$$= -(y - p'\gamma)\ \hat{p}^{-1}(\hat{\beta} - \beta\ \beta')\hat{p}^{-1}$$

$$= (Q_p + q_y\ q');$$

$$Q_p\ p = -(y - p'\gamma)\hat{p}^{-1}\beta\ \hat{p}^{-1}p - \hat{p}^{-1}\beta\ \gamma' p$$

$$= -(y - p'\gamma)\ \hat{p}^{-1}\beta - \hat{p}^{-1}\ \beta\ \gamma' p = -\ y\ \hat{p}^{-1}\beta$$

$$= -\ q_y\ y.$$

That the budget constraint is satisfied is apparent from

$$p'q = p'\gamma + (y - p'\gamma)p'\hat{p}^{-1}\beta = p'\gamma + (y - p'\gamma) = y.$$

We have seen that Stone's linear expenditure system is derivable from maximization of a particular utility function. In fact, it is the only linear expenditure system which can be derived from a classical utility function. The proof, which is due to Stone (1954), will be sketched here to illustrate the power of the classical restrictions developed in Section 2. A general linear expenditure system would take the form

$$\hat{p}\ q = \alpha + y\ \beta + A\ p$$

with

$$\alpha = (\alpha_1, \ldots, \alpha_n)' , \qquad \beta = (\beta_1, \ldots, \beta_n)'$$

$$A = \begin{pmatrix} \alpha_{11} & \cdots & \alpha_{1n} \\ \vdots & & \vdots \\ \alpha_{n1} & \cdots & \alpha_{nn} \end{pmatrix}$$

being fixed parameters. Stone's linear expenditure system is the special case in which $\alpha = 0$, $\iota'\beta = 1$, $A = (I - \beta\iota')\hat{\gamma}$. In the general system the demand functions are

$$q = \hat{p}^{-1}\ (\alpha + y\ \beta + A\ p)$$

so that

$$q_y = \hat{p}^{-1}\beta$$

$$Q_p = \hat{p}^{-1} A - \hat{p}^{-1} (\hat{\alpha} + y\,\hat{\beta} + \hat{A}p)\hat{p}^{-1}.$$

Then

$$p'q_y = p'\hat{p}^{-1}\beta = \iota'\beta,$$

whence imposition of (2.15a) -- $p'q_y = 1$ -- yields

$$\iota'\beta = 1,$$

as in Stone's system. Continuing,

$$Q_p'p = A'\iota - \hat{p}^{-1}(\hat{\alpha} + y\,\hat{\beta} + \hat{A}p)\iota$$

$$= A'\iota - \hat{p}^{-1}(\alpha + y\,\beta + A\,p)$$

$$= A'\iota - q,$$

whence imposition of (2.16a) -- $Q_p'p = -q$ -- yields

$$A'\iota = 0$$

as in Stone's system, where

$$A'\iota = \hat{\gamma}\,(I - \iota\,\beta')\iota = \hat{\gamma}\,(\iota - \iota) = 0.$$

Continuing,

$$q_y\,q' = \hat{p}^{-1}\beta(\alpha + y\,\beta + A\,p)'\,\hat{p}^{-1},$$

so

$$Q_p + q_yq' = \hat{p}^{-1}[A\hat{p} - \hat{\alpha} - y\hat{\beta} - \hat{A}p + \beta\alpha' + y\beta\beta' + \beta p'A']\hat{p}^{-1}$$

(3.9) $$= -y\,\hat{p}^{-1}(\hat{\beta} - \beta\beta')\hat{p}^{-1} + \hat{p}^{-1}(A\hat{p} - \hat{A}p + \beta p'A')\hat{p}^{-1}$$

$$- \hat{p}^{-1}(\hat{\alpha} - \beta\alpha')\hat{p}^{-1}.$$

Imposition of (2.17a) -- $(Q_p + q_y q')' = Q_p + q_y q'$ -- requires that (3.9) be symmetric. Of the three terms on the right of (3.9) the first is automatically symmetric, and symmetry of the third requires

$$\alpha = 0$$

as in Stone's system.[11] This leaves the second term; specifically we must have

$$A \hat{p} - A\hat{}p + \beta p'A' = \hat{p} A' - A\hat{}p + A p \beta' .$$

That is

$$A \hat{p} - A p \beta' = \hat{p} A' - \beta p'A'$$

or

$$A \hat{p} (I - \iota\beta') = (I - \beta\iota')\hat{p} A' .$$

The only way to obtain this is to have

$$A = (I - \beta\iota')\hat{\gamma}$$

where $\hat{\gamma}$ may be any diagonal matrix. And this, as we have seen, is just the feature of Stone's system.

In summary, we have found that imposing the classical constraints on

$$\hat{p} q = \alpha + y \beta + A p$$

results in

$$\hat{p} q = y \beta + (I - \beta\iota')\hat{\gamma} p$$

where $\iota'\beta = 1$ and γ is arbitrary. Thus Stone's linear expenditure system is indeed the only linear expenditure system derivable from a classical utility function.[12]

Returning to Stone's system, we now focus on the behavior of the average budget shares as income varies, prices being given. Multiplying (3.4) by y^{-1}, we obtain the average budget share vector

$$w = y^{-1}\hat{p}\, q = y^{-1}\, \hat{p}\, \gamma + y^{-1}(y - p'\gamma)\beta$$

$$= (y^{-1}p'\gamma)[(p'\gamma)^{-1}\hat{p}\, \gamma] + y^{-1}(y - p'\gamma)\beta$$

$$= \quad \alpha \qquad w^* \qquad + (1 - \alpha) \quad \beta,$$

say; algebraically

(3.10) $\quad w_i = \alpha\, w_i^* + (1-\alpha)\beta_i \qquad\qquad (i = 1,\ldots,n).$

Here $\alpha = p'\gamma/y$ is the ratio of subsistence income to income and $(1-\alpha) = (y-p'\gamma)/y$ is its complement, the ratio of supernumerary income to income; $w_i^* = p_i\gamma_i/p'\gamma$ are the "subsistence budget shares" which give the composition of expenditures by a consumer whose income is at the subsistence level $p'\gamma$; and $w^* = (w_1^*,\ldots,w_n^*)'$ is the "subsistence budget share vector." From (3.10) we see that at any income level y, the average budget share w_i is a weighted average of the subsistence budget share w_i^* and the marginal budget share β_i, the weights being the ratios of subsistence income and supernumerary income to income, respectively. At subsistence income $y = p'\gamma$, $\alpha = 1$ and $1 - \alpha = 0$, so that all the weight is on w_i^*: the average budget shares are just the subsistence budget shares. As income rises, α falls and $1 - \alpha$ rises, the weight shifting to the marginal budget shares. As income grows indefinitely large, the average budget shares approach the (constant) marginal budget shares. The linear expenditure system -- as does any model with linear Engel curves -- thus makes a neat distinction between the composition of expenditures at low and high income levels.

Now consider the income elasticities $\eta_i = \beta_i/w_i$. As income rises from subsistence level, w_i moves from w_i^* toward β_i, so that η_i moves from β_i/w_i^* toward 1. The path of the income elasticity is rising, constant, or falling according as β_i is less than, equal to, or greater than w_i^*. The classification of goods into luxuries, neutrals, and necessities remains unchanged over the income range (although it may depend on prices). Again these are consequences of Engel curve linearity.

3.2 Utility Aspects of the Demand Functions

Inserting q = q(y, p) from (3.5) into the u(q) of (3.1) we find the indirect utility function of the present model:

$$u = u^*(y, p) = \beta' \log [(y - p'\gamma)\, \hat{p}^{-1}\beta]$$

$$= \beta' \log \beta + \log (y - p'\gamma) - \beta' \log p. \qquad (3.11)$$

Algebraically

$$u^*(y, p) = \textstyle\sum_i \beta_i \log \beta_i + \log (y - \sum_i p_i \gamma_i) - \sum_i \beta_i \log p_i .$$

Thus the marginal utility of income is

$$\lambda = u^*_y = \partial u^*/\partial y = (y - p'\gamma)^{-1}$$

as indeed had been shown at (3.3). The vector of marginal utilities of prices is

$$u^*_p = \partial u^*/\partial p = - [(y - p'\gamma)^{-1}\gamma + \hat{p}^{-1}\beta]$$

which, incidentally, equals $-\lambda\, q$ in accordance with (2.20).

Consider the marginal utility of income function $\lambda = \lambda(y, p) = (y - p'\gamma)^{-1}$. Its income and price slopes are given by

$$\lambda_y = -(y - p'\gamma)^{-2} \qquad \lambda_p = (y - p'\gamma)^{-2}\,\gamma. \qquad (3.12)$$[13]

The income elasticity of λ is

$$\eta_{\lambda y} = \lambda_y\, \lambda^{-1}\, y = -\, y(y - p'\gamma)^{-1}.$$

This parameter has an intuitive interpretation in the present model, which is better seen in terms of its reciprocal, the income flexibility

$$\phi = -\,(y - p'\gamma)/y\ ,$$

or rather in terms of the absolute value of ϕ,

$$|\phi| = (y - p'\gamma)/y\ .$$

For $|\phi|$ is just the ratio of supernumerary income to income, which we met as $1 - \alpha$ at the end of Section 3.1. The decomposition (3.10) may thus be written

$$w_i = (1 - |\phi|)\ w^* + |\phi|\ \beta_i.$$

The "supernumerary ratio" $(y - p'\gamma)/y$ would seem to be a natural welfare indicator in the present model -- it rises from 0 to 1 as y rises from $p'\gamma$ to ∞ with prices given. Since $\eta_{\lambda y}$ is the negative of the reciprocal of $(y - p'\gamma)/y$, it also rises with income, thus making plausible Frisch's proposed use of it as a welfare indicator; more on this in Section 3.5.

An exact expression for the true cost of living index -- one which holds in the large as well as the small -- may be found in the present model; see Klein and Rubin (1947), Samuelson (1947b), Geary (1949). The supernumerary ratio again appears as a key parameter. Start from an initial income-price situation with y^o, $p^o = (p_1^o, \ldots, p_n^o)'$, and utility level

$$u^o = u^*(y^o, p^o) = \textstyle\sum_i \beta_i \log \beta_i + \log(y^o - \sum_i p_i^o \gamma_i) - \sum_i \beta_i \log p_i^o.$$

If prices change to $p^1 = (p_1^1, \ldots, p_n^1)$, then the resulting change in utility as a function of income is

$$\Delta u = \log (y - p^{1\prime}\gamma) - \log (y^o - p^{o\prime}\gamma) - \beta'(\log p^1 - \log p^o),$$

so that y*, the income required to maintain utility (obtained by setting $\Delta u = 0$) satisfies

$$\log [(y^* - p^{1\prime}\gamma)/(y^o - p^{o\prime}\gamma)] = \textstyle\sum_i \beta_i \log (p_i^1/p_i^o).$$

Taking antilogs and then rearranging:

$$y^* = p^{1\prime}\gamma + (y^o - p^{o\prime}\gamma) \prod_{i=1}^{n} (p_i^1/p_i^o)^{\beta_i}$$

$$= y^o \left\{ \left[\frac{p^{o\prime}\gamma}{y^o}\right] \left[\frac{p^{1\prime}\gamma}{p^{o\prime}\gamma}\right] + \left[\frac{y^o - p^{o\prime}\gamma}{y^o}\right] \left[\prod_{i=1}^{n} (p_i^1/p_i^o)^{\beta_i}\right] \right\}.$$

The expression in curly brackets, $y^*/y^o = T$, say, is thus the true cost of living index, which may be written out as

$$(3.13) \quad T = (1 - |\phi^o|) \sum_i w_i^{*o} P_i + |\phi^o| \Pi_i P_i^{\beta_i} ,$$

where

$|\phi^o| = (y^o - p^{o\prime}\gamma)/y^o$ is the supernumerary ratio

in the initial situation;

$w_i^{*o} = p_i^o \gamma_i / \sum_j p_j^o \gamma_j$ $(i = 1,...,n)$ are the sub-

sistence budget shares in the initial situation; and

$P_i = p_i^1/p_i^o$ $(i = 1,...,n)$ are the price relatives.

In (3.13), the true cost of living index is displayed as a weighted arithmetic mean of two price indexes. The first price index, $\sum_i w_i{}^{*o} P_i$, is a weighted arithmetic mean of the price relatives, the weights being the subsistence budget shares. The second price index, $\prod_{i=1}^{n} P_i^{\beta_i}$, is a weighted geometric mean of price relatives, the weights being the marginal budget shares. These two price indexes are then combined into T, their weights being the subsistence ratio (= 1 minus supernumerary ratio) and the supernumerary ratio, respectively.

In contrast to conventional cost of living indexes, T takes correct account of the substitution which accompanies price changes. Consider the Laspeyre price index

$$L = \sum_i w_i^o P_i$$

where

$$w_i^o = p_i^o q_i^o / y^o .$$

From (3.10) we have

$$w_i^o = (1 - |\phi^o|) w_i^{*o} + |\phi^o| \beta_i ,$$

so that in the present model

$$L = (1 - |\phi^o|)\sum_i w_i^{*o} P_i + |\phi^o| \sum_i \beta_i P_i \quad ,$$

which differs from T only in using an arithmetic rather than a geometric mean in its second component. In view of the familiar inequality between arithmetic and geometric means, we see that

$$L \geqslant T$$

(with equality holding if and only if $P_1 = \ldots = P_n = P$, say, in which case $L = T = P$). This illustrates the well-known upward bias of the Laspeyre price index.

Equation (3.13) also illustrates one of the points made in the passage quoted from Frisch: The true cost-of-living index is a function (of initial income) rather than a scalar. For consumers close to subsistence the first term on the right of (3.13) dominates: heavy weight is given to changes in the prices of goods which have high subsistence budget shares. For consumers far from subsistence the second term on the right dominates: heavy weight is given to changes in the prices of goods which have high marginal budget shares. The true cost of living index may well differ between workmen and ambassadors.

In the present model, the first order conditions could be solved for $q = q(y, p)$ and $\lambda = \lambda(y, p)$ explicitly. Thus the fundamental matrix expressions for differentials of q and λ, which were exploited in the general theory of Chapter 2, have been bypassed in Chapter 3. Nevertheless, it is instructive to illustrate the general theory with the present model. To facilitate this we first use (3.5) to rewrite the second derivative matrix in Stone's system as

$$U = - (\hat{q} - \hat{\gamma})^{-1}\hat{\beta} \, (\hat{q} - \hat{\gamma})^{-1}$$

$$= - [(y - p'\gamma) \, \hat{p}^{-1}\hat{\beta}]^{-1}\hat{\beta} \, [(y - p'\gamma)\hat{p}^{-1}\hat{\beta}]^{-1}$$

$$(3.14) \qquad = - (y - p'\gamma)^{-2} \, \hat{p} \, \hat{\beta}^{-1}\hat{p},$$

the inverse of which is

$$(3.15) \qquad U^{-1} = -(y - p'\gamma)^2 \, \hat{p}^{-1}\hat{\beta} \, \hat{p}^{-1}.$$

Now the general results (2.11) - (2.14) may be checked out. Pre- and post-multiply (3.15) by p' and p respectively:

$$p'U^{-1}p = -(y - p'\gamma)^{-2}\ \iota'\hat{\beta}\ \iota = -\ (y - p'\gamma)^{2}$$

since $\iota'\hat{\beta}\ \iota = \iota'\beta = 1$. Therefore

$$(p'U^{-1}p)^{-1} = -\ (y - p'\gamma)^{-2} = \lambda_y$$

in view of (3.12). This illustrates (2.11). Continuing, we compute

$$\begin{aligned}\lambda\ q_y + \lambda_y\ q &= (y - p'\gamma)^{-1}\hat{p}^{-1}\beta \\ &\quad -\ (y - p'\gamma)^{-2}\ [\gamma + (y - p'\gamma)\hat{p}^{-1}\beta] \\ &= -\ (y - p'\gamma)^{-2}\gamma \\ &= -\ \lambda_p\end{aligned}$$

using in turn (3.3), (3.7), (3.12), (3.5), and again (3.12). This illustrates (2.12). Next we compute

$$\lambda_y\ U^{-1}p = -(y - p'\gamma)^{-2}[-(y - p'\gamma)^{2}\hat{p}^{-1}\hat{\beta}\ \hat{p}^{-1}]\ p = \hat{p}^{-1}\beta = q_y$$

using in turn (3.12), (3.15), and (3.7). This illustrates (2.13). Finally we compute

$$\begin{aligned}\lambda U^{-1} - \lambda\lambda_y^{-1}q_y q_y' - q_y q' &= (y - p'\gamma)^{-1}[-(y - p'\gamma)^{2}\hat{p}^{-1}\ \hat{\beta}\ \hat{p}^{-1}] \\ &\quad -\ (y - p'\gamma)^{-1}[-(y - p'\gamma)^{2}]\hat{p}^{-1}\beta\beta'\hat{p}^{-1} \\ &\quad -\ \hat{p}^{-1}\beta[\gamma + (y - p'\gamma)\hat{p}^{-1}\beta]' \\ &= -(y - p'\gamma)\hat{p}^{-1}\hat{\beta}\ \hat{p}^{-1} - \hat{p}^{-1}\beta\ \gamma' \\ &= Q_p\end{aligned}$$

using in turn (3.3), (3.15), (3.13), (3.7), (3.5), and (3.8). This illustrates (2.14).

We complete this section by computing the income elasticity and marginal budget share vectors; price coefficients will be taken up in Section 3.3. Since

$$q_y = \hat{p}^{-1}\beta ,$$

the marginal budget share vector is simply

$$\mu = \hat{p}\, q_y = \beta;$$

algebraically

$$\mu_i = \beta_i \qquad (i = 1,\ldots,n).$$

Since the average budget share vector is

$$w = y^{-1}\hat{p}\, q = (1 + \phi)w^* - \phi\, \beta,$$

the income elasticity vector is

$$\eta = \hat{w}^{-1}\mu = [(1 + \phi)\hat{w}^* - \phi\, \hat{\beta}]^{-1}\beta;$$

algebraically

$$\eta_i = \beta_i/[w_i^* - \phi\, (\beta_i - w_i^*)] \qquad (i = 1,\ldots,n).$$

Note that as is the case with any directly additive utility function, inferior goods are ruled out: q_y and hence μ and η are all positive.

3.3 Additive Utility

The Stone-Geary utility function is directly additive, so that one may rely on the theory of Section 2.3 to derive, for the linear expenditure system, all the price coefficient matrices in terms of the income coefficient vectors and the income flexibility ϕ. Alternatively, the price coefficient matrices could be derived directly by manipulating q_y and Q_p; in that event the results would serve to illustrate the additivity theory.

We start with

$$q_y = \hat{p}^{-1}\beta$$

$$\mu = \beta$$

$$\phi = -(y - p'\gamma)y^{-1},$$

and proceed to utilize the theorems of Section 2.3. For the uncompensated price slope matrix we find

$$\begin{aligned} Q_p &= \phi\, y\, \hat{q}_y\, \hat{p}^{-1} - q_y(q + \phi\, y\, q_y)' \\ &= \phi\, y\, \hat{p}^{-1}\hat{\beta}\, \hat{p}^{-1} - \hat{p}^{-1}\beta\,(\gamma - \phi\, y\, \hat{p}^{-1}\beta + \phi\, y\, \hat{p}^{-1}\beta)' \\ &= \phi\, y\, \hat{p}^{-1}\hat{\beta}\, \hat{p}^{-1} - \hat{p}^{-1}\beta\, \gamma' \end{aligned}$$

as indeed we had at (3.8). For the utility-compensated price slope matrix, we find

$$\begin{aligned} Q_p^* &= \phi\, y\, \hat{q}_y\,(\hat{p}^{-1} - \iota\, q_y') \\ &= \phi\, y\, \hat{p}^{-1}\, \hat{\beta}(\hat{p}^{-1} - \iota\, \beta'\hat{p}^{-1}) \\ &= \phi\, y\, \hat{p}^{-1}(\hat{\beta} - \beta\, \beta')\, \hat{p}^{-1}; \end{aligned}$$

algebraically

$$(\partial q_i/\partial p_j)^* = \begin{cases} \phi\, y\, p_i^{-2}\, \beta_i(1 - \beta_i) & \text{if } i = j \\ -\phi\, y\, p_i^{-1}p_j^{-1}\, \beta_i\, \beta_j & \text{if } i \neq j. \end{cases}$$

Note that in the present system, as in any directly additive one, all goods are Hicks-Allen substitutes: with $\phi < 0$, $\beta_i > 0$, and $\beta_j > 0$, clearly $(\partial q_i/\partial p_j)^* > 0$ for all $i \neq j$.

For the marginal-utility-of-income-compensated price slope matrix,

$$Q_p^{**} = \phi\, y\, \hat{p}^{-1}\hat{q}_y = \phi\, y\, \hat{p}^{-1}\hat{\beta}\, \hat{p}^{-1} ;$$

algebraically

$$(\partial q_i/\partial p_j)^{**} = \begin{cases} \phi \; y \; p_i^{-2}\beta_i & \text{if } i = j \\ 0 & \text{if } i \neq j. \end{cases}$$

Note that in the present system, as in any directly additive one, all specific substitution effects are zero: $(\partial q_i/\partial p_j)^{**} = 0$ for all $i \neq j$.

For the uncompensated price elasticity matrix,

$$\begin{aligned} H &= \phi \; \hat{\eta} - \eta \; w'(I + \phi \; \hat{\eta}) \\ &= \phi \; \hat{\eta} - \eta(w' + \phi \; w'\hat{\eta}) \\ &= \phi \; \hat{\eta} - \eta(w + \phi \; \beta)' \\ &= \phi \; \hat{\eta} - \eta(y^{-1} \; \hat{p} \; \gamma)'; \end{aligned}$$

algebraically

$$\eta_{ij} = \begin{cases} \eta_i(\phi - y^{-1}p_i\gamma_i) & \text{if } i = j \\ -\eta_i y^{-1} p_j \gamma_i & \text{if } i \neq j. \end{cases}$$

In the present model, each uncompensated own-price elasticity must lie between 0 and -1 -- so that demand is price-inelastic in the usual sense -- cf. Stone (1965, p. 285). This may be shown as follows:

$$\begin{aligned} \eta_{ii} &= \eta_i(\phi - y^{-1}p_i\gamma_i) = -\eta_i y^{-1}[(y - p'\gamma) + p_i\gamma_i] \\ &= -\eta_i y^{-1}[\beta_i^{-1}p_i(q_i - \gamma_i) + p_i\gamma_i] \\ &= -\eta_i y^{-1}[\beta_i^{-1}p_i q_i + (1 - \beta_i^{-1})p_i\gamma_i] \\ &= -\beta_i p_i^{-1} q_i^{-1} y \; y^{-1}[\beta_i^{-1}p_i q_i + (1 - \beta_i^{-1})p_i\gamma_i] \\ &= -1 + (1 - \beta_i) \; q_i^{-1}\gamma_i \; . \end{aligned}$$

With $0 < \beta_i < 1$ and $0 \leqslant \gamma_i < q_i$, it must be the case that $-1 \leqslant n_{ii} < 0$.

For the utility-compensated price elasticity matrix,

$$H^* = \phi\ \hat{\eta} - \phi\ \eta\ w'\hat{\eta} = \phi\ \hat{\eta}(I - \iota\ \beta');$$

algebraically

$$\eta^*_{ij} = \begin{cases} \phi\ \eta_i(1 - \beta_i) & \text{if } i = j \\ -\ \phi\ \eta_i\ \beta_j & \text{if } i \neq j. \end{cases}$$

Each utility-compensated own-price elasticity must lie between 0 and 1:

$$\eta^*_{ii} = \phi\ \eta_i(1 - \beta_i) = -(y - p'\gamma)y^{-1}\beta_i p_i^{-1} q_i^{-1}\ y(1 - \beta_i)$$

$$= -p_i(q_i - \gamma_i)\ p_i^{-1} q_i^{-1}(1 - \beta_i)$$

$$= -\ (1 - \beta_i)\ (1 - q^{-1}\gamma_i).$$

With $0 < \beta_i < 1$ and $0 \leqslant \gamma_i < q_i$, clearly $-1 < \eta^*_{ii} < 0$.

For the marginal-utility-of-income-compensated price elasticity matrix we find

$$H^{**} = \phi\ \hat{\eta}\quad ;$$

algebraically

$$\eta^{**}_{ij} = \begin{cases} \phi\ \eta_i & \text{if } i = j \\ 0 & \text{if } i \neq j. \end{cases}$$

Each marginal-utility-of-income-compensated own-price elasticity must lie between 0 and 1:

$$\eta^{**}_{ii} = \phi\ \eta_i = -(y - p'\gamma)y^{-1}\beta_i p_i^{-1} q_i^{-1} y$$

$$= -\ p_i(q_i - \gamma_i)\ p_i^{-1} q_i^{-1}$$

$$= -\ (1 - q_i^{-1}\gamma_i);$$

since $0 \leq \gamma_i < q_i$, clearly $-1 \leq \eta^*_{ii} < 0$.

Turning to the price response matrices, we find

$$\Theta = \phi\,(\hat{\mu} - \mu\,\mu') - \mu\,w'$$

$$= \phi\,(\hat{\beta} - \beta\,\beta') - \beta\,w'$$

$$= \phi\,\hat{\beta} - \beta\,(\phi\,\beta + w)'$$

$$K = \phi\,(\hat{\mu} - \mu\,\mu') = \phi\,(\hat{\beta} - \beta\,\beta')$$

$$N = \phi\,\hat{\mu} = \phi\,\hat{\beta};$$

algebraically the last two are

$$\kappa_{ij} = \begin{cases} \phi\,\beta_i(1 - \beta_i) & \text{if } i = j \\ -\phi\,\beta_i\beta_j & \text{if } i \neq j \end{cases}$$

$$\nu_{ij} = \begin{cases} \phi\,\beta_i & \text{if } i = j \\ 0 & \text{if } i \neq j \end{cases} .$$

The economy of parameterization which is associated with directly additive utility is apparent in Stone's linear expenditure system, which after all uses only $2n - 1$ independent parameters. These are the $n - 1$ independent elements of β (recall $\iota'\beta = 1$) and the n elements of γ.

3.4 Monotonic Transformations of the Utility Function

The present model offers an opportunity to illustrate the effect of monotonic transformations of the utility function. Consider the antilog of Stone-Geary utility:

$$v = e^u = \prod_{i=1}^{n} (q_i - \gamma_i)^{\beta_i}.$$

Since $v_u = dv/du = e^u = v = v_{uu} = dv_u/du$, we have

$$v_q = \partial v/\partial q = v_u u_q = v\ (\hat{q} - \hat{\gamma})^{-1}\beta = v(y - p'\gamma)^{-1}p$$

and

$$V = \partial v_q/\partial q' = v_u\ U + v_{uu}\ u_q u_q'$$

$$= v[-(\hat{q} - \hat{\gamma})^{-1}\hat{\beta}(\hat{q} - \hat{\gamma})^{-1} + (\hat{q} - \hat{\gamma})^{-1}\beta\ \beta'(\hat{q} - \hat{\gamma})^{-1}]$$

$$= -\ v[(\hat{q} - \hat{\gamma})^{-1}(\hat{\beta} - \beta\ \beta')(\hat{q} - \hat{\gamma})^{-1}]$$

$$= -\ v(y - p'\gamma)^{-2}\hat{p}\ \hat{\beta}^{-1}(\hat{\beta} - \beta\ \beta')\hat{\beta}^{-1}\hat{p}.$$

The transformation has of course changed the marginal utilities, but they remain positive, $v_q > 0$. The ratios of the marginal utilities, that is the marginal rates of transformation of the goods, are unchanged. As for the second derivative matrix, it still displays diminishing marginal utility to each good, but is no longer diagonal nor is it negative definite. The elements of V are

$$v_{ij} = \begin{cases} -\ v(y - p'\gamma)^{-2}p_i^2(1 - \beta_i)\beta_i^{-1} & \text{if } i = j \\ v(y - p'\gamma)^{-2}p_i p_j & \text{if } i \neq j, \end{cases}$$

and V is, like $-(\hat{\beta} - \beta\ \beta')$, nonpositive definite of rank $n - 1$.

The indirect utility function is

$$v = v^*(y,\ p) = \exp[u^*(y,p)] = (y - p'\gamma)\ \prod_{i=1}^{n} (\beta_i/p_i)^{\beta_i}.$$

The marginal utility of income under v is

$$\kappa = \partial v/\partial y = v_u\ \lambda = v(y - p'\gamma)^{-1}$$

which is still positive. The income slope of the marginal utility of income is

$$\kappa_y = \partial\kappa/\partial y = v_u\lambda_y + \lambda^2 v_{uu} = v(\lambda_y + \lambda^2)$$
$$= v[-(y - p'\gamma)^{-2} + (y - p'\gamma)^2]$$
$$= 0,$$

so that the income elasticity of the marginal utility of income is also zero:

$$\eta_{\kappa y} = 0.$$

This demonstrates with particular force the fact that the proposed welfare indicator is not invariant under non-linear monotonic transformations.

3.5 Welfare Indicators

Frisch's proposed welfare indicator $\eta_{\lambda y}$ has intuitive appeal in the present model, provided that we agree to focus on the original, Stone-Geary, utility function. The marginal utility of income $\lambda = (y - p'\gamma)^{-1}$ then has the hyperbolic form described on p. 37 above, and indeed $\eta_{\lambda y} = -(y - p'\gamma)^{-1} y$ rises monotonically with income (from $-\infty$ to -1) in accord with Frisch's conjecture.

We have seen that the supernumerary ratio $(y - p'\gamma)/y$, being the negative of the reciprocal of $\eta_{\lambda y}$ in the present model, provides an equivalent (in the ordinal sense) welfare indicator. This supernumerary ratio may also be interpreted in terms of the composition of expenditures. We have mentioned that the proportion of income spent on food is a frequently used (inverse) indicator of welfare; equivalently one might use its complement -- the proportion spent on non-food goods as a (positive) indicator. In the same spirit, one might classify goods into essentials and nonessentials, and use the proportion of income spent on essentials as an (inverse) welfare indicator; equivalently, the complementary proportion spent on non-essentials might be used as a (positive) indicator. In this same spirit, we may in Stone's system distinguish between subsistence and supernumerary expenditures on each good -- $p_i\gamma_i$ and $\beta_i(y - p'\gamma)$ respectively -- rather than between essential and nonessential goods. Then $\sum_i p_i \gamma_i / y$, measuring the proportion of income spent on subsistence, would serve as an (inverse) welfare indicator; equivalently the complementary proportion $(y - \sum_i p_i \gamma_i)/y$ would serve as a (positive) welfare indicator. And this last proportion is just the supernumerary ratio, equal to $-\eta_{\lambda y}^{-1}$ in the present model.

We conclude that the interpretation of Frisch's proposed welfare indicator is enriched when the Stone-Geary utility function applies.

3.6 Further Comments

Stone's linear expenditure system has been explored in some detail here, in part to illustrate various aspects of the general classical theory of consumer demand. As a framework for a cross-country comparison of complete sets of demand functions, it has some attractions. Empirical implementation is facilitated by linearity of the expenditure functions, although these functions are nonlinear in the parameters. Being built up from a utility function, the system has a built-in economy of parameters. The parameters have a convenient interpretation, and one might even argue that the Stone-Geary direct utility function is plausible per se.

The fact that the underlying utility function is directly additive means that Stone's system is not appropriate when a fine classification of goods is involved.[14] The further fact that the Engel curves are linear means that the system is not applicable when wide variation in incomes are observed, as in a cross-section. Neither of these limitations would seem to be confining for the type of data we use. In any case, Stone's linear expenditure system is one of the few explicit functional forms for a complete set of demand functions which have been derived from a utility function, and is thus one of the few which are known to be consistent with a classical utility maximization process. Both its direct and indirect utility functions are known explicitly.[15]

Before turning to other functional forms, we mention several other aspects of the present model.

(a) The Cobb-Douglas Case: If $\gamma = 0$ in the Stone-Geary utility function, then we have the special "Cobb-Douglas" case:

$$u = \beta' \log q.$$

The expenditure functions simplify to

$$\hat{p}\, q = y\, \beta,$$

so that the average budget shares are identical with the marginal budget shares:

$$w = y^{-1}\hat{p}\, q = \beta.$$

That is to say, the composition of the budget is independent of income (as well as of prices); in other words all income elasticities are unity. The demand functions are

$$q_i = \beta_i(y/p_i) \qquad (i = 1,\ldots,n),$$

so that all Cournot own-price elasticities are - 1 and all Cournot cross-price elasticities are 0. The indirect utility function is

$$u^* = \textstyle\sum_i \beta_i \log \beta_i + \sum \beta_i \log (y/p_i). \qquad (3.16)$$

The marginal utility of income is

$$\lambda = y^{-1} ,$$

the income elasticity of which is

$$\eta_{\lambda y} = -1$$

at all income levels. The Cobb-Douglas case is empirically useless, but is of theoretical interest in that it depicts a preference ordering -- the only one -- which is simultaneously directly and indirectly additive.[16]

(b) Aggregation: Working with aggregate data, it is useful to recognize that the linear expenditure system aggregates perfectly over individuals within a "nation". Suppose that each consumer, m = 1, ..., M, has the same Stone-Geary utility function. That is, the <u>mth</u> consumer maximizes

$$u^m = \beta' \log (q^m - \gamma)$$

subject to his budget constraint

$$y^m = p'q^m,$$

the superscript m labelling the utility, quantity demanded, and income of the <u>mth</u> consumer. We have assumed that β, γ, and p are the same for all consumers and we further assume that all consumers are above subsistence:

$$y^m - p'\gamma > 0 \qquad (m = 1, \ldots, M).$$

Expenditures by the <u>mth</u> consumer are then given by

$$\hat{p}\, q^m = p\, \gamma + (y^m - p'\gamma)\beta.$$

Summing over consumers will give national expenditures, which for convenience we express in per capita terms by dividing through by M:

$$\hat{p} \sum_m q^m = \hat{p} \sum_m \gamma + \sum_m (y^m - p'\gamma)\beta,$$

that is

$$\hat{p}\, \bar{q} = \hat{p}\, \gamma + (\bar{y} - p'\gamma)\beta$$

where $\bar{q} = \sum_m q^m/M$ and $\bar{y} = \sum_m y^m/M$ are national quantity and national income, respectively, measured in per capita terms. Thus the aggregation is perfect, the nation as a whole displaying a linear expenditure system with the same parameters as each of its constituents has.

It is apparent that these national (per capita) expenditure functions would result also from maximizing a national (per capita) utility function

$$\bar{u} = \beta' \log(\bar{q} - \gamma)$$

subject to the national (per capita) budget constraint

$$\bar{y} = p'\bar{q}.$$

The consumer sector as a whole, in other words, behaves "as if" it were maximizing a single community utility function (taking income and prices as given!). Apart from prices, the per capita quantity demanded depends only on mean (per capita) income, and not on the distribution of income; this is also clear from the linearity of the individual expenditure functions.

The "as if" utility function may be distinguished from the function which gives per capita utility obtained in the consumer sector.[17] The latter does depend on the income distribution, since the marginal utility of income does vary with income. Specifically,

$$\begin{aligned}\bar{u}^* &= M^{-1}\textstyle\sum_m u^*(y^m, p)\\ &= M^{-1}\textstyle\sum_m\sum_i\beta_i \log \beta_i + M^{-1}\sum_m \log (y^m - p'\gamma)\\ &\qquad - M^{-1}\textstyle\sum_m\sum_i \beta_i \log p_i\\ &= \textstyle\sum_i \beta_i \log(\beta_i/p_i) + \overline{\log z}\end{aligned}$$

where $z^m = y^m - p'\gamma$ and $\overline{\log z} = M^{-1}\sum_m \log z^m$. Clearly $\bar{u}^*$ is not a function of $\bar{y}$ alone, but rather depends on the income distribution. If supernumerary income, z, is log-normally distributed with expectation $\bar{z}$ and variance σ_z^2 (in which case mean income is $\bar{y} = \bar{z} + p'\gamma$ and the variance of income is $\sigma_y^2 = \sigma_z^2$) then

$$\overline{\log z} = \log\, (\bar{y} - p'\gamma)^2\ [(\bar{y} - p'\gamma)^2 + \sigma_y^2]^{-½},$$

and the derivative of $\bar{u}^*$ with respect to the variance of the income distribution, prices and mean income being given, is

$$\partial\bar{u}^*/\partial\sigma_y^2 = -½\ [(\bar{y} - p'\gamma)^2 + \sigma_y^2]^{-1} < 0.$$

(c) Constants in the Differential Demand Functions: For Stone's system, we have the exact demand functions $q = q(y, p)$; the constants in these functions are β and γ. As indicated in Section 2.2, some recent empirical work has relied on differential versions of the demand functions:

e.g., dlog q as a function of dlog y and dlog p. Alternative formulations have been used, distinguished by their selection of coefficients to be treated as constants: e.g., η and H, or μ and N. For possible comparisons with these other formulations, we may characterize Stone's system as follows. As to the income coefficients, it takes μ as constant (recall $\mu = \beta$). As to the price coefficients, we may say that it takes as constant

$$\hat{p}\ (Q_p - Q_p^{**}) = \hat{q}\ \hat{p}\ (H - H^{**})\ \hat{p}^{-1} = y\ (\theta - N)\hat{p}^{-1},$$

since each of these equals $- \beta\ \gamma'$, which is constant in Stone's system. An alternative characterization is that Stone's system takes as constant $\mu = \beta$ and $q + \phi\ y\ q_y = \gamma$.

4
ALTERNATIVE FUNCTIONAL FORMS

4.1 Quadratic Utility Function

A model of consumer demand may be developed from the quadratic utility function

(4.1) $u = \alpha' q - \frac{1}{2} q' B q,$

in which the parameters are

$$\alpha = (\alpha_1, \ldots, \alpha_n)'$$

$$B = \begin{pmatrix} \beta_{11} & \cdots & \beta_{1n} \\ \vdots & & \vdots \\ \beta_{n1} & & \beta_{nn} \end{pmatrix},$$

it being assumed that $\alpha > 0$, that B is positive definite, and that the function is defined only where $\alpha - B q > 0$ and $q > 0$. While quadratic utility has been featured in the literature on decision making under uncertainty it has received less attention in consumer demand analysis; but see Allen and Bowley (1935), Theil (1961, pp. 387-395), and Theil (1967, pp. 183-188, 228-229).

To derive the complete set of demand functions, we start with

$$u_q = \partial u / \partial q = \alpha - B q.$$

This explains the restriction on the domain, $\alpha - B\,q > 0$, since the classical theory requires $u_q > 0$; the restriction $q > 0$ is also inherent in the classical theory.

The second derivative matrix is

$$(4.2) \qquad U = \partial u_q/\partial q' = -B,$$

which is negative definite by assumption, as required. Setting $u_q = \lambda\,p$ gives

$$\alpha - B\,q = \lambda\,p.$$

Premultiplying by B^{-1} and rearranging gives

$$(4.3) \qquad q = B^{-1}(\alpha - \lambda\,p),$$

which after premultiplication by p' and use of $p'q = y$ shows the marginal utility of income function $\lambda = \lambda(y, p)$ to be

$$(4.4) \qquad \lambda = (p'B^{-1}p)^{-1}(p'B^{-1}\alpha - y).$$

Inserting this into (4.3) gives the demand functions $q = q(y, p)$:

$$(4.5) \quad q = B^{-1}\alpha - (p'B^{-1}p)^{-1}(p'B^{-1}\alpha - y)\,B^{-1}p.$$

The expenditure functions are

$$(4.6) \qquad \hat{p}\,q = \hat{p}\,B^{-1}\alpha - (p'B^{-1}p)^{-1}(p'B^{-1}\alpha - y)\,\hat{p}\,B^{-1}p.$$

Provided we suspend reason for the moment, an interpretation for this system may be offered, which is something of a mirror image of that provided for the linear expenditure system. Over the domain for which the function is defined, $u_q > 0$, so that $\lambda > 0$; thus from (4.4),

$$y < p'B^{-1}\alpha.$$

One might think, therefore, of $p'B^{-1}\alpha$ as "bliss income." A consumer at that income level would, according to (4.5), "buy" $\sum_j \beta^{1j}\alpha_j$ of good 1, ..., $\sum_j \beta^{nj}\,\alpha_j$ of good n, where β^{ij} denotes the i, j element of B^{-1}. At prices $p_1,\ldots,p_n$ these "maximum tolerable quantities" would cost

$\sum_i p_i \sum_j \beta^{ij} \alpha_j = p'B^{-1}\alpha$, exhausting the bliss income. A consumer with income y below the bliss level cannot "afford" this package; he has an "infrabliss deficit" of $p'B^{-1}\alpha - y > 0$. He behaves as if he first "bought" the maximum tolerable quantities, and then reduced his expenditures down to his income level by "selling back" goods, financing his infrabliss deficit in the "proportions" $p_i \sum_j \beta^{ij} p_j / p'B^{-1}p$. At the conclusion of this series of conceptual transactions he will, on balance, have spent

$$p_i \sum_j \beta^{ij} \alpha_j - (p'B^{-1}p)^{-1}(p'B^{-1}\alpha - y) p_i \sum_i \beta^{ij} p_j$$

on the ith good and this is indeed the ith row of (4.6). Such an interpretation, however, is tenuous at best, which accounts for the proviso that reason be suspended and for the liberal sprinkling of quotation marks. The condition $y < p'B^{-1}\alpha$, while necessary, is by no means sufficient for operation of the model. Even for $y < p'B^{-1}\alpha$, the demand functions (4.5) may call for negative quantities of some goods, thus violating the requirement $q > 0$. Also, elements of $B^{-1}\alpha$ may be negative (which casts doubt on their interpretation as quantities) and elements of $B^{-1}p$ may be negative (which casts doubt on the interpretation

of the elements of $(p'B^{-1}p)^{-1}\hat{p}B^{-1}p$ as proportions). With u_q being linear in q, some goods may have negative marginal utility at low income levels and others may have negative marginal utility at high income levels, all within the range $0 < y < p'B^{-1}\alpha$, if the consumer were actually obeying (4.5). Houthakker (1953) develops the demand system which results when inequality conditions are properly taken into account: goods enter and depart the budget as income changes. Our classical approach, however, requires that all goods are in the budget, thus effectively restricting the y, p domain over which the model applies. We proceed with reference to the restricted domain over which all goods are in the budget. The demand functions (4.5) then hold.[18]

Returning to the demand functions $q = q(y,p)$, we find the income slope vector

$$q_y = (p'B^{-1}p)^{-1}B^{-1}p \; ; \tag{4.7}$$

algebraically

$$(\partial q_i / \partial y) = (p'B^{-1}p)^{-1} \sum_j \beta^{ij} p_j \qquad (i = 1,\ldots,n).$$

As was true in the linear expenditure system, the income slopes do not involve income, so that Engel curves are again linear. However, the slopes do involve prices. As noted above, elements of $B^{-1}p$ may be negative, so that inferior goods are now permitted. In other words, the marginal budget shares $\mu_i = (p'B^{-1}p)^{-1}p_i\sum_j\beta^{ij}p_j$ $(i = 1,\ldots,n)$, while summing to 1, are not necessarily bounded between 0 and 1.

The price slope matrix is

$$(4.8) \qquad Q_p = \partial q/\partial p' = (p'B^{-1}p)^{-1}(y - p'B^{-1}\alpha)B^{-1}$$
$$- 2(p'\beta^{-1}p)^{-2}(y - p'B^{-1}\alpha)B^{-1}pp'B^{-1}$$
$$- (p'B^{-1}p)^{-1}B^{-1}p\ \alpha'B^{-1}\ .$$

A wide variety of price coefficients are possible under the quadratic utility function.

The indirect utility function, obtained by substitution of (4.5) into (4.1) and collection of terms, is

$$(4.9) \qquad u^*(y, p) = \tfrac{1}{2}\ [\alpha'B^{-1}\alpha - (p'B^{-1}p)^{-1}(p'\beta^{-1}\alpha - y)^2].$$

The marginal utility of income function $\lambda = \lambda(y, p)$ is thus

$$\lambda = \partial u^*/\partial y = (p'\beta^{-1}p)^{-1}(p'\beta^{-1}\alpha - y),$$

as indeed we had found at (4.4). The income slope of $\lambda = \lambda(y, p)$ is

$$\lambda_y = -\ (p'B^{-1}p)^{-1}\ ;$$

this conforms with (2.11) since $U = -\ B$. The income elasticity of the marginal utility of income is

$$\eta_{\lambda y} = -\ (p'B^{-1}\alpha - y)^{-1}y\ ;$$

its reciprocal, the income flexibility, is

$$\phi = -\ (p'B^{-1}\alpha - y)/y.$$

Both of these are negative over the relevant income range, $0 < y < p'B^{-1}\alpha$.

However, $\eta_{\lambda y}$ shows perverse behavior as a welfare indicator, falling from 0 to $-\infty$ as income rises from 0 to the bliss level $p'B^{-1}\alpha$, prices being given. To be sure, $\eta_{\lambda y}$ is monotonic in income, so it may serve as an inverse welfare indicator.[19]

The average budget shares are given by

$$(4.10) \quad w = y^{-1}\hat{p}\, q = y^{-1}(p'B^{-1}\alpha)(p'B^{-1}\alpha)^{-1}\hat{p}\, B^{-1}\alpha$$

$$- y^{-1}(p'B^{-1}\alpha - y)(p'B^{-1}p)^{-1}\hat{p}\, B^{-1}p$$

$$= (1 - \phi)\, \overline{w} + \phi\, \mu$$

where

$w = (p'B^{-1}\alpha)^{-1}\hat{p}\, B^{-1}\alpha$ is the "bliss budget share vector," and

$\mu = (p'B^{-1}p)^{-1}\hat{p}\, B^{-1}p$ is the marginal budget share vector.

While (4.10) resembles the decomposition provided for Stone's system in (3.10), its interpretation is troublesome for the reasons indicated in our interpretation of the demand functions.

For the quadratic utility function, a true cost of living index may be derived. Starting from an initial situation y^o, p^o, let prices change to p^1. The resulting change in utility as a function of income may be read off from the indirect utility function (4.9) as

$$\Delta u = -\tfrac{1}{2}[(p^{1\prime}B^{-1}p^1)^{-1}(p^{1\prime}B^{-1}\alpha - y)^2$$

$$- (p^{o\prime}B^{-1}p^o)^{-1}(p^{o\prime}B^{-1}\alpha - y^o)^2].$$

This may be set at zero and solved for $y = y^*$, the utility-maintaining income in the new price situation. After arrangement one finds

$$y^* = p^{1\prime}B^{-1}\alpha - (p^{o\prime}B^{-1}\alpha - y^o)\ (p^{1\prime}B^{-1}p^1/p^{o\prime}B^{-1}p^o)^{\frac{1}{2}}$$

$$= y^o\ \{(1 - \phi^o)\ \textstyle\sum_i \overline{w}_i\ P_i + \phi^o\pi\}$$

where

$-\phi^o = (p^{o\prime}B^{-1}\alpha - y^o)/y^o$ is the infrabliss ratio in the initial situation;

$\bar{w}_i^o = p_i^o \sum_j \beta^{ij} \alpha_j / p^{o\prime} B^{-1} \alpha$ $(i = 1,\ldots,n)$ are the bliss budget shares in the initial situation;

$P_i = p_i^1/p_i^o$ $(i = 1,\ldots,n)$ are the price relatives; and

$\pi = (p^{1\prime} B^{-1} p^1 / p^{o\prime} B^{-1} p^o)^{\frac{1}{2}}$ is a quadratically weighted price index.

The true cost-of-living index is thus

$$(4.11) \qquad T = y^*/y^o = (1 - \phi^o)\sum_i \bar{w}_i^o P_i + \phi^o \pi ,$$

which has a formal resemblance to the true cost of living index (3.13) of Stone's system. However an interpretation of (4.11) is awkward, for reasons suggested earlier in this section.

We consider several further aspects of the quadratic utility function.

Since $u_q = \alpha - B\,q$, under a quadratic utility function the marginal rate of substitution between any two goods is the ratio of linear functions of quantities:

$$\frac{u_i}{u_j} = \frac{\alpha_i - \beta_{i1}q_1 - \ldots - \beta_{in}q_n}{\alpha_j - \beta_{j1}q_1 - \ldots - \beta_{jn}q_n} \quad (i,\ j = 1,\ldots,n).$$

These are invariant under monotonic transformations of the utility function. If marginal rates of transformation are ratios of linear functions of income quantities, then a preference ordering is said to be a <u>linear preference scale</u>, following Allen and Bowley (1935, pp. 109-112, 135-137). The quadratic utility function thus is an example of a linear preference scale; it is special in that the coefficients are symmetrical, i.e. $\beta_{ij} = \beta_{ji}$ $(i,\ j = 1,\ldots,n)$. As Allen and Bowley (1935, p. 137) show, if the preference scale is linear, then the Engel curves are also linear.

A special case of the quadratic utility function obtains when B is diagonal, for then utility is directly additive:

$$u = \sum_i \alpha_i q_i - \tfrac{1}{2} \sum_i \beta_{ii}\, q_i^2 = \sum_i u^i(q_i)$$

where $u^i(q_i) = \alpha_i q_i - \frac{1}{2}\beta_{ii} q_i^2$. The additive quadratic function is associated with Gossen; see Samuelson (1947a, p. 93) and Allen and Bowley (1935, p. 139). The demand functions (4.5) specialize to

$$q_i = \frac{\alpha_i}{\beta_{ii}} + \frac{p_i/\beta_{ii}}{\sum_j p_j/\beta_{jj}}\, y - \frac{p_i/\beta_{ii}}{\sum_j p_j/\beta_{jj}} \sum_k p_k \alpha_k/\beta_{kk};$$

and income flexibility is

$$\phi = 1 - \frac{\sum_i p_i \alpha_i \beta_{ii}^{-1}}{y}.$$

Returning to the general quadratic utility function, we remark that its attraction as a basis for a complete set of demand functions is limited. To be sure, the utility function has some direct appeal, as is evident from its use in decision theory. It does allow for inferiorities, complementarities, and specific substitution effects, so that it may be appropriate when a fine classification of goods is employed.

However, the resulting demand functions are quite complex, inhibiting estimation. Indeed the system (4.5) has not, to our knowledge, ever been estimated. This complexity is suppressed in decision models when the constraint coefficients which correspond to p are treated as constants. The resulting decision rules are linear, corresponding to the linear Engel curves in the present consumer demand context.

4.2 Direct Addilog Utility Function

Some work has been done on a model of consumer demand based on the direct addilog utility function

$$u = \sum_{i=1}^{n} \alpha_i q_i^{\beta_i} \qquad (4.12)$$

in which the parameters are

$$(\alpha_1, \ldots, \alpha_n)' = \alpha$$

$$(\beta_1, \ldots, \beta_n)' = \beta,$$

it being assumed that $\alpha > 0$, $\iota'\alpha = 1$, $\iota > \beta > 0$. This function was introduced by Houthakker (1960a, pp. 252-256).

The marginal utilities and second derivatives are given by

$$u_i = \alpha_i \beta_i \, q_i^{(\beta_i - 1)} \tag{4.13}$$

$$u_{ij} = \begin{cases} \alpha_i \beta_i (\beta_i - 1) \, q_i^{(\beta_i - 2)} & \text{if } i = j \\ 0 & \text{if } i \neq j \end{cases}; \tag{4.14}$$

utility being directly additive as the name suggests. Note that marginal utilities are everywhere positive and diminishing. The first order conditions $u_q = \lambda p$ are algebraically

$$\alpha_i \beta_i q_i^{(\beta_i - 1)} = \lambda \, p_i$$

or

$$\gamma_i \, q_i^{(\beta_i - 1)} = \lambda \, p_i \qquad (i = 1,\ldots,n), \tag{4.15}$$

where we have defined

$$\gamma_i = \alpha_i \, \beta_i \qquad (i = 1,\ldots,n).$$

Multiplying (4.15) by q_i and then summing over i gives

$$\lambda = y^{-1} \textstyle\sum_i \gamma_i q_i^{\beta_i}, \tag{4.16}$$

which however does not give $\lambda = \lambda(y, p)$ explicitly. Substituting (4.16) back into (4.15) would not give $q = q(y, p)$ explicitly, and indeed the explicit solution for the complete set of demand functions generated by direct addilog utility is unknown. As a consequence the explicit solution for the indirect utility function $u = u^*(y, p)$ is also unknown.

Following Houthakker (1960a, p. 253) we acquire a partial solution by dividing the first-order conditions in pairs to get

$$\gamma_i q_i^{(\beta_i-1)} / \gamma_j q_j^{(\beta_j-1)} = p_i/p_j \quad (i \neq j;\ i,\ j = 1,\ldots,n),$$

which may be rewritten as

(4.17) $$(1-\beta_i) \log q_i - (1-\beta_j) \log q_j = \log(\gamma_i/\gamma_j) - \log(p_i/p_j) \quad (i \neq j;\ i,\ j = 1,\ldots,n).$$

The literature contains few statements about the properties of the demand functions which result from direct addilog utility. One is Houthakker's (1960a, p. 253) remark that ratios of income elasticities are constant. We may establish this along with several other properties as follows. The differential of (4.17) is

(4.18) $$(1-\beta_i) \text{dlog } q_i - (1-\beta_j) \text{dlog } q_j = - \text{dlog } p_i + \text{dlog } p_j.$$

Suppose y changes, with p fixed; then

$$(1-\beta_i) \text{dlog } q_i - (1-\beta_j) \text{dlog } q_j = 0,$$

which upon division by dlog y yields

(4.19) $$\eta_i/\eta_j = (1-\beta_j)/(1-\beta_i).$$

Suppose p_i changes, with y and all other elements of p (including p_j) fixed; then

$$(1-\beta_i) \text{dlog } q_i - (1-\beta_j) \text{dlog } q_j = - \text{dlog } p_i,$$

which upon division by dlog p_i yields

(4.20) $$(1-\beta_i)\eta_{ii} = - 1 + (1-\beta_j)\eta_{ji} \quad (i \neq j;\ i,\ j = 1,\ldots,n).$$

For the special case of the direct addilog utility function which has $\beta_1 = \ldots = \beta_n = \beta$, say, more explicit results are available. The first-order conditions specialize to

$$(4.21) \quad \gamma_i\, q_i^{(\beta-1)} = \lambda\, p_i \quad (i = 1,\ldots,n).$$

Multiplication by $p_i^{-\beta}$ gives

$$p_i^{-\beta}\gamma_i = \lambda\, (p_i q_i)^{(1-\beta)} ,$$

which may be raised to the power $(1-\beta)^{-1}$ to give

$$(4.22) \quad (p_i^{-\beta}\gamma_i)^{(1-\beta)^{-1}} = \lambda^{(1-\beta)^{-1}}\, p_i q_i ,$$

which in turn may be summed over i to give

$$(4.23) \quad \sum_i (p_i^{-\beta}\gamma_i)^{(1-\beta)^{-1}} = \lambda^{(1-\beta)^{-1}} y.$$

Dividing (4.22) by (4.23) and then multiplying by y/p_i we find the complete set of demand functions $q = q(y, p)$:

$$(4.24) \quad q_i = \frac{(p_i/\gamma_i)^{(\beta-1)^{-1}}}{\sum_j p_j (p_j/\gamma_j)^{(\beta-1)^{-1}}}\, y \qquad (i = 1,\ldots,n).$$

All Engel curves are straight lines through the origin so that all income elasticities are unity.[20]

Returning to (4.23) we obtain the marginal utility of income function $\lambda = \lambda(y, p)$ for the special direct addilog utility function:

$$\lambda = y^{-(1-\beta)} \left[\sum_i (p_i^{-\beta}\gamma_i)^{(1-\beta)^{-1}}\right]^{(1-\beta)}.$$

It follows immediately that

$$\eta_{\lambda y} = \beta - 1$$

which is negative but independent of the level of income.

4.3 Indirect Addilog Utility Function

It is possible to base models of consumer demand upon indirect rather than direct utility functions. The derivation may well be simpler in view of the fact that if $u = u^*(y, p)$, then

(4.25) $q = q(y, p) = -(u_y^*)^{-1} u_p^* = -\lambda^{-1} u_p^*$;

algebraically

$$q_i = -(\partial u^*/\partial p_i)/(\partial u^*/\partial y) = -\lambda^{-1}(\partial u^*/\partial p_i) \qquad (i = 1,\dots,n).$$

This relation, which is known as Roy's identity, is obvious from (2.20) above, and enables one to write down explicit demand functions after differentiating the indirect utility function. Since u_y^* and u_p^* are functions of y and p alone, one finds q as a function of y and p alone, that is the complete set of demand functions, $q = q(y, p)$.

Assuming that the indirect utility function $u^*(y, p)$ is continuous and repeatedly differentiable, we consider some expressions for the income and price slopes of the demand functions. The matrix of second derivatives of $u^*(y, p)$ will be written as

$$\begin{pmatrix} \partial u_p^*/\partial p' & \partial u_p^*/\partial y \\ \partial u_y^*/\partial p' & \partial u_y^*/\partial y \end{pmatrix} = \begin{pmatrix} U^* & \lambda_p \\ \lambda_p' & \lambda_y \end{pmatrix},$$

where we have defined the symmetric n x n matrix U^* whose i,j element is $u_{ij}^* = \partial^2 u^*/\partial p_i \partial p_j$, and have used the previous result $u_y^* = \lambda$ which implies that $(\partial u_y^*/\partial p') = \lambda_p' = (\partial u_p^*/\partial y)'$ and $(\partial u_y^*/\partial y) = \lambda_y$. Differentiating (4.25) with respect to y we obtain the income slope vector as

(4.26) $q_y = -\lambda^{-1}(\partial u_p^*/\partial y) - \lambda^{-2}\lambda_y u_p^* = -\lambda^{-1}(\lambda_p + \lambda_y q)$

which is simply a rearrangement of (2.12). Next we differentiate (4.25) with respect to p' to obtain the price slope matrix as

$$(4.27) \quad Q_p = -\lambda^{-1}U^* - \lambda^{-2}u^*_p\,\lambda'_p = -\lambda^{-1}(U^* + q\,\lambda'_p);$$

algebraically

$$(4.28) \quad (\partial q_i/\partial p_j) = -\lambda^{-1}\,[u^*_{ij} + q_i(\partial\lambda/\partial p_j)] \qquad (i, j = 1, \ldots, n)$$

which is equation (18) in Houthakker (1960a). Inserting the transpose of (2.12) into (4.27) gives

$$(4.29) \quad Q_p = -\lambda^{-1}U^* + \lambda^{-1}\lambda_y\,q\,q' + q\,q'_y$$

which may be viewed as a sort of dual to (2.14).[21]

Presumably for reasons of analytical convenience, attention has been concentrated upon the situation where utility is <u>indirectly additive</u>, that is where

$$(4.30) \quad u = u^*(y, p_1, \ldots, p_n) = \sum_{i=1}^{n} u^{*i}(y/p_i),$$

each $u^{*i}(\;\;)$ being a function of only the corresponding y/p_i.[22] In this situation, $u^*_{ij} = 0$ for all $i \neq j$, i.e., U^* is a diagonal matrix. As Houthakker (1960a, pp. 250-251) demonstrates, indirect additivity imposes substantial restrictions among the price and income slopes. If we postmultiply the transpose of (4.27) by p and draw on the previous results that $Q'_p\,p = -q$ and $q'p = y$ we would find in general that

$$q = \lambda^{-1}(U^*\,p + \lambda_p\,y).$$

Under indirect additivity this implies that

$$(4.31) \quad q_j = \lambda^{-1}[u^*_{jj}p_j + y\,(\partial\lambda/\partial p_j)] \qquad (j = 1, \ldots, n),$$

that is,

$$(4.32) \quad \lambda^{-1}(\partial\lambda/\partial p_j) = q_j/y - (p_j/y)(u^*_{jj}/\lambda) \quad (j = 1, \ldots, n).$$

Inserting this into (4.28) for $i \neq j$, we find that under indirect additivity

$$(4.33)\quad (\partial q_i/\partial p_j) = q_i\ [(p_j/y)(u^*_{jj}/\lambda) - (q_j/y)]$$

$$(i \neq j;\ i,j = 1,\ldots,n),$$

so that

$$(4.34)\quad (\partial q_i/\partial p_j)/(\partial q_k/\partial p_j) = q_i/q_k$$

$$(i \neq j,\ k \neq j;\ i,j,k = 1,\ldots,n),$$

while in elasticity terms

$$(4.35)\quad \eta_{ij} = (p_j^2/y)(u^*_{jj}/\lambda) - w_j \quad (i \neq j;\ i,j = 1,\ldots,n).$$

These last four equations are (19)-(22) in Houthakker (1960a). Under indirect additivity, we see, Cournot cross-price slopes are proportional to quantities, regardless of which price is changing, or in other words, Cournot cross-price elasticities depend only on the good whose price is changing and not upon the good whose quantity is responding. As Houthakker shows, this condition is sufficient as well as necessary for indirect additivity.

Turning to the Cournot own-price slope, we have from (4.28) with $i = j$,

$$(\partial q_i/\partial p_i) = -\lambda^{-1}u^*_{ii} - \lambda^{-1}q_i(\partial\lambda/\partial p_i),$$

while from (4.31)

$$q_i/p_i = \lambda^{-1}u^*_{ii} + \lambda^{-1}(y/p_i)(\partial\lambda/\partial p_i).$$

Adding these and then multiplying by p_i/q_i gives

$$\begin{aligned}\eta_{ii} + 1 &= \lambda^{-1}[(y/q_i) - p_i]\ (\partial\lambda/\partial p_i)\\ &= \lambda^{-1}(y/q_i)(1 - w_i)(\partial\lambda/\partial p_i)\\ &= -\lambda^{-1}(y/q_i)(1 - w_i)[\lambda(\partial q_i/\partial y) + \lambda_y\ q_i]\\ (4.36)\qquad &= -(1 - w_i)(\eta_i + \eta_{\lambda y}) \quad (i = 1,\ldots,n),\end{aligned}$$

using the definitions $\eta_{ii} = (p_i/q_i)(\partial q_i/\partial p_i)$,

$w_i = p_i q_i/y$, $\eta_i = (y/q_i)(\partial q_i/\partial y) = (p_i/w_i)(\partial q_i/\partial y)$,

$\eta_{\lambda y} = \lambda^{-1} \lambda_y y$, along with the ith element of (2.12).[23]

Note that $\eta_{\lambda y}$ once again appears as a key parameter.

While this discussion has dealt with indirect additivity in general terms, empirical work has in fact been confined to a particular case, namely the indirect addilog utility function

$$(4.37) \qquad u = u^*(y, p) = \sum_{i=1}^{n} \alpha_i (y/p_i)^{\beta_i}$$

in which the parameters are

$$(\alpha_1, \ldots, \alpha_n) = \alpha' ,$$

$$(\beta_1, \ldots, \beta_n) = \beta' ,$$

it being assumed that $0 > \alpha$, $-\iota'\alpha = 1$, and $0 > \beta > -\iota$. This function was proposed and implemented by Houthakker (1960a, pp. 252-256; 1960b); the demand functions which result had already been explored by Somermeyer and Wit (1956). Somermeyer, Hilhorst, and Wit (1961), Russell (1965), and Parks (1966, 1969) have applied the model to data on the Netherlands, U.S.A., and Sweden, respectively.

To obtain the demand functions generated by indirect addilog utility, we may proceed as follows. Differentiating (4.37) with respect to y gives the marginal utility of income function

$$(4.38) \qquad \lambda = u^*_y = \sum_k \alpha_k \beta_k p_k^{-\beta_k} y^{(\beta_k - 1)} = y^{-1}[\sum_k \alpha_k \beta_k (y/p_k)^{\beta_k}],$$

while differentiating with respect to $p_1, \ldots, p_n$ gives

$$(4.39) \qquad (\partial u^*/\partial p_i) = - p_i^{-1} \alpha_i \beta_i (y/p_i)^{\beta_i} \qquad (i = 1, \ldots, n).$$

Then application of Roy's identity immediately gives the demand functions:

$$(4.40) \qquad q_i = -\lambda^{-1}(\partial u^*/\partial p_i) = \frac{\alpha_i \beta_i (y/p_i)^{1+\beta_i}}{\sum_k \alpha_k \beta_k (y/p_k)^{\beta_k}} \quad (i = 1, \ldots, n)$$

which is equation (29) in Houthakker (1960a) -- or with a redefinition of parameters, equation (12) of Houthakker (1960b).

The features of this demand system may be spelled out as follows. First, note that the average budget shares, obtained by multiplying (4.40) through by p_i/y, are

$$(4.41) \qquad w_i = [\textstyle\sum_k \alpha_k \beta_k (y/p_k)^{\beta_k}]^{-1} [\alpha_i \beta_i (y/p_i)^{\beta_i}] \qquad (i = 1,\ldots,n).$$

Now take the logarithm of (4.40) to obtain

$$(4.42) \qquad \log q_i = \log(\alpha_i \beta_i) + (1 + \beta_i) \log (y/p_i) - \log \textstyle\sum_k \alpha_k \beta_k (y/p_k)^{\beta_k} \qquad (i = 1,\ldots,n).$$

The elasticities are then found by differentiating (4.42). For the income elasticities we find

$$(4.43) \qquad \eta_i = (1 + \beta_i) - [\textstyle\sum_k \alpha_k \beta_k (y/p_k)^{\beta_k}]^{-1} [\textstyle\sum_k \alpha_k \beta_k^2 (y/p_k)^{\beta_k}]$$
$$= (1 + \beta_i) - \textstyle\sum_k \beta_k w_k \qquad (i = 1,\ldots,n)$$

using (4.41); and similarly for the price elasticities we find

$$(4.44) \qquad \eta_{ij} = \begin{cases} -(1 + \beta_i) + \beta_i w_i & \text{if } i = j \\ \beta_j w_j & \text{if } i \neq j \end{cases} \qquad (i,j=1,\ldots,n)$$

Note that differences between income elasticities are constant in the present model. Note also that, as is true in any indirectly additive model, cross-price elasticities do not depend on the good whose quantity is responding -- i.e., η_{ij} is the same for all $i \neq j$.[24]

Turning to the welfare indicator, differentiating (4.38) with respect to y gives

$$\lambda_y \doteq \partial\lambda/\partial y = y^{-1} \textstyle\sum_k \alpha_k \beta_k^2 (y/p_k)^{\beta_k} y^{-1} - y^{-2} \textstyle\sum_k \alpha_k \beta_k (y/p_k)^{\beta_k}$$
$$= y^{-2} \textstyle\sum_k \alpha_k \beta_k (\beta_k - 1)(y/p_k)^{\beta_k}$$

$$= y^{-2}\sum_k(\beta_k-1)w_k \, \lambda \, y$$

(4.45) $$= y^{-1}\lambda \sum_k(\beta_k-1)w_k,$$

using (4.38) and (4.41). The income elasticity of the marginal utility of income is thus

(4.46) $$\eta_{\lambda y} = \lambda_y \, y \, \lambda^{-1} = \sum_k(\beta_k-1)w_k = -1 + \sum_k \beta_k w_k.$$

It is not hard to see that this measure follows Frisch's conjecture, rising with y when p is given. For as income rises, the high income elasticity goods occupy a larger share of the budget; but these are precisely the goods which have large β's -- see (4.43). Thus as income rises the weighted average $\sum_k \beta_k w_k$ is increasingly dominated by the higher β's; i.e., $\sum_k \beta_k w_k$ rises with income, and thus $\eta_{\lambda y}$ does also.[25]

Now consider the true cost of living index under indirect addilog utility. Starting from an initial situation y^o, p^o, let prices change to p^1. The resulting change in utility as a function of income may be read off from (4.37) as

$$\Delta u = \sum_i \alpha_i \, (y/p_i^1)^{\beta_i} - \sum_i \alpha_i \, (y^o/p_i^o)^{\beta_i}.$$

Setting this at zero determines the utility-maintaining income y* by

$$\sum_i \alpha_i[(y^*/p_i^1)^{\beta_i} - (y^o/p_i^o)^{\beta_i}] = 0,$$

that is, by

(4.47) $$\sum_i \alpha_i(y^o/p_i^o)^{\beta_i}[(T/P_i)^{\beta_i} - 1] = 0,$$

where $T = y^*/y^o$ is the true cost of living index and the $P_i = p_i^1/p_i^o$ $(i = 1,\ldots,n)$ are the price relatives. We can divide (4.47) through by $\sum_k \alpha_k \beta_k(y^o/p_k^o)^{\beta_k}$ which equals

$\alpha_i\beta_i(y^o/p_i^o)^{\beta_i}/w_i^o$ according to (4.41) and then rewrite (4.47) as

$$\sum_i (w_i^o/\beta_i)[(T/P_i)^{\beta_i} - 1] = 0.$$

We have not succeeded in finding either an interpretation or an explicit solution for T from this equation.

The attractions of the indirect addilog utility function as a basis for a consumer demand model are not overwhelming. It certainly does impose restrictions on the demand equations, utilizing only 2n - 1 independent parameters. However, it does not appear possible to justify indirect additivity by appeal to intuition, in the way that was done for direct additivity. The direct utility function which generates indirect addilog utility is not known explicitly. Empirical implementation of the model has been inhibited by the fact that the demand -- or expenditure -- functions are nonlinear in the parameters. Houthakker (1960b, p. 5) arrived at the indirect addilog demand system by adjusting a traditional constant elasticity system $q_i = a_i\ (y/p_i)^{bi}$ in order to satisfy the budget constraint $\sum_i p_i q_i = y$. It seems unfortunate that the adjustment failed to preserve the ease of estimation which is a key attraction of the constant elasticity model. In practice, Houthakker (1960a, 1960b) suppressed the non-linearity by considering ratios of quantities

$$q_i/q_j = (\alpha_i\beta_i/\alpha_j\beta_j)(y/p_i)^{\beta_i}(y/p_j)^{\beta_j}.$$

Taking logarithms gives

$$\log q_i - \log q_j = \alpha^*_{ij} + \beta_i \log(y/p_i) - \beta_j \log (y/p_j)$$

where $\alpha^*_{ij} = \log (\alpha_i\beta_i/\alpha_j\beta_j)(i,\ j = 1,\ldots,n)$; this is a convenient linear form. Of course, when it is estimated for goods taken in pairs, n - 1 estimates of each β_i are obtained. Houthakker (1960a, p. 256; 1960b, p. 11) suggested that the similarity of the alternative estimates of the same parameter provides a test of the indirect addilog model. It remained for Parks (1969) to establish an appropriate way to handle the nonlinearity -- that is to impose the constraints that the $\beta_1,\ldots,\beta_n$ do not change across equations. In brief, his procedure is to estimate jointly the (n-1)-equation system

$$\log q_1 - \log q_j = \alpha^*_{1j} + \beta_1 \log(y/p_1) - \beta_j \log(y/p_j) \qquad (j = 2,\ldots,n).^{26}$$

4.4 Powell's "Model of Additive Preferences"

Each of the sets of demand functions treated in Chapters 3 and 4 rested solidly on a classical utility-maximizing base: for some specific choice of utility function, the set gave exactly the quantities demanded as functions of income and prices. We now turn to consumer demand models which have a more pragmatic flavor: the functional form of the demand equations is specified directly, then interpreted and restricted in the light of consumer demand theory.

Alan Powell has developed an ingenious variant of Stone's linear expenditure system; estimates are reported in Powell (1965, 1966) and Powell et al. (1968). Consider the general linear expenditure system discussed in Section 3.1:

$$\hat{p}\, q = y\, \beta + A\, p.^{27} \qquad (4.48)$$

In such a system, the demand functions, income slopes, and price slopes will be given by

$$q = \hat{p}^{-1}(y\, \beta + A\, p)$$

$$q_y = \hat{p}^{-1}\, \beta$$

$$Q_p = \hat{p}^{-1}[A - (y\, \hat{\beta} + A\hat{\ }p)\, \hat{p}^{-1}] = \hat{p}^{-1}(A - \hat{q}).$$

Thus

$$A = \hat{p}\, Q_p + \hat{q}. \qquad (4.49)$$

If utility is directly additive, then by the basic theorem given earlier, also

$$(4.50) \quad Q_p = \phi\, y\, \hat{q}_y\, (\hat{p}^{-1} - \iota\, q_y') - q_y\, q'.$$

Combining these two equations we find

$$\begin{aligned} A &= \phi\, y\, \hat{q}_y\, (I - p\, q_y') - \hat{p}\, q_y\, q' + \hat{q} \\ &= \phi\, y\, \hat{q}_y - \phi\, y\, \hat{p}\, q_y\, q_y' - \hat{p}\, q_y\, q' + \hat{q} \\ &= (I - \hat{p}\, q_y\, \iota')(\hat{q} + \phi\, y\, \hat{q}_y) \\ &= (I - \beta\iota')(\hat{q} + \phi\, y\, \hat{\beta}\, \hat{p}^{-1}). \end{aligned}$$

With both A and β being constant, the assumption of direct additivity requires that $\hat{q} + \phi\, y\, \hat{\beta}\, \hat{p}^{-1}$ be constant.[28] However, we might impose that assumption only <u>approximately</u>, requiring merely that

$$A = (I - \beta\iota')(\hat{\bar{q}} + \phi\, y\, \hat{\beta}\, \hat{\bar{p}}^{-1})$$

$$(4.51) \quad = (I - \beta\iota')(\hat{\bar{q}} - \sigma\, \hat{\beta}\, \hat{\bar{p}}^{-1})$$

where $\bar{q} = (\bar{q}_1, \ldots, \bar{q}_n)'$ and $\bar{p} = (\bar{p}_1, \ldots, \bar{p}_n)'$ are the vectors of sample mean quantities and prices, and where $\sigma = -\phi\, y$ is taken as constant. This indeed is Powell's proposal. Substituting (4.51) into (4.48) we find, after some rearrangement,

$$(4.52) \quad \hat{p}\, q = \hat{p}\, \bar{q} + (y - p'\bar{q})\, \beta - \sigma\hat{\beta}\, (I - \iota\beta')\, \dot{p},$$

where $\dot{p} = (p_1/\bar{p}_1, \ldots, p_n/\bar{p}_n)'$ is the vector of price relatives, and where we have used $\iota'\beta = p'q_y = 1$.

This expenditure system, corresponding to equation (11) of Powell (1966), is his "model of additive preferences." Algebraically it may be written as

$$(4.53) \quad p_i q_i = p_i \bar{q}_i + \beta_i (y - \textstyle\sum_j p_j \bar{q}_j) - \sigma\beta_i [(p_i/\bar{p}_i) - \textstyle\sum_j \beta_j (p_j/\bar{p}_j)] ,$$

whereupon an interpretation becomes available. Given y, $p_1, \ldots, p_n$, the consumer first purchases "typical quantities" $\bar{q}_1, \ldots, \bar{q}_n$ of the goods. This leaves him "supernumerary income" of $y - \sum_j p_j \bar{q}_j$, which he allocates in the proportions $\beta_1, \ldots, \beta_n$. Up to this point, the interpretation parallels that for Stone's system, with the observable $\bar{q}$'s playing the role of the parameter γ's. However, this allocation of income is modified to reflect substitution effects which arise from changes in relative prices, in accord with the last of the three terms on the right of (4.53). The budget constraint is preserved after this modification since the last term sums to zero over i, a result most readily seen in the matrix version (4.52), where $\iota'\hat{\beta}\ (I - \iota\beta') = \beta'(I - \iota\beta') = (\beta' - \beta') = 0$ since $\iota'\beta = 1$.

Or, following Powell's argument further, we may note that deflation of $(y - \sum_j p_j \bar{q}_j)$ and of

$$\{p_i q_i - p_i \bar{q}_i + \sigma\, \beta_i\ [(p_i/\bar{p}_i) - \sum_j \beta_j (p_j/\bar{p}_j)]\}$$

by p_i

> would yield respectively a measure of "real" supernumerary income in terms of purchasing power of the ith good, and a quantity index for the ith commodity. Very roughly, then, the method is equivalent to fitting quantities adjusted for movements in relative prices as a linear function of "uncommitted" real income.
>
> Powell (1966, p. 663).

Powell's model departs from Stone's in several respects. Since $\bar{q}$ is observable, the model contains just n parameters -- the n - 1 independent elements of β, and σ -- rather than 2n - 1. The parameter σ, which at the sample mean point equals $-\phi\ y$, is taken as constant in the model, while in Stone's model $-\phi\ y = (y - p'\gamma)$ is a critical variable. Price and income responses are similar in structure to those in Stone's model; in particular Engel curves are linear. However the restrictions of classical consumer demand theory have been imposed only approximately; in particular symmetry of Slutsky price slopes will hold only at points where $p_i p_j = \bar{p}_i \bar{p}_j$ (cf. Powell (1966, p. 664)).

From a purely statistical point of view there are attractions to attempting to account, by variations in income, for variations in the q_i about their sample means $\bar{q}_i$, rather than about their "minimum" values γ_i. An iterative computational scheme for fitting the model (which is nonlinear in the parameters) appears to converge more rapidly than the fitting method used by Stone, although no direct comparative experience is known to me. For analytical purposes it appears to be an open question whether the gain in parameter economy is worth the sacrifice of a strict utility-maximizing foundation. It is worth emphasizing that the point at which Powell imposes additive utility restrictions approximately is the very point at which imposition of general utility restrictions exactly led to Stone's linear expenditure system.

What does seem to have gone unnoticed is that Powell's model can in fact be obtained exactly from maximizing a Stone-Geary utility function provided that the minimum required quantities are known to satisfy a particular pattern. Suppose that for the period under consideration the utility function is

$$(4.54) \quad u = \beta' \log(q - \gamma)$$

where

$$(4.55) \quad \gamma = \bar{q} - \sigma \hat{\bar{p}}^{-1} \beta,$$

$\bar{q}$ and $\bar{p}$ being the observed sample mean quantity and price vectors and σ and β being unknown parameters (with $0 < \beta < \iota$ and $\iota'\beta = 1$).[29] Maximization of (4.54) with p and $y = p'q$ given yields the familiar expression

$$\hat{p}\, q = \hat{p}\, \gamma + (y - p'\gamma)\, \beta,$$

which upon inserting (4.55) becomes

$$\hat{p}\,\hat{q} = \hat{p}\,(\bar{q} - \sigma\,\hat{\bar{p}}^{-1}\beta) + [y - p'(\bar{q} - \sigma\,\hat{\bar{p}}^{-1}\beta)]\beta$$

$$= \hat{p}\,\bar{q} + (y - p'\bar{q})\beta - \sigma[\hat{\dot{p}}\,\beta - (\dot{p}'\beta)\beta]$$

$$= \hat{p}\,\bar{q} + (y - p'\bar{q})\beta - \sigma\,(\hat{\beta}\,\dot{p} - \beta\,\beta'\dot{p})$$

$$(4.56)\qquad = \hat{p}\,\bar{q} + (y - p'\bar{q})\beta - \sigma\,\hat{\beta}(I - \iota\beta')\,\dot{p},$$

which is just Powell's model (4.52).[30]

On this analysis, furthermore, the income flexibility is

$$\phi = -(y - p'\gamma)/y = -(y - p'\bar{q} + \sigma\,\dot{p}'\beta)/y,$$

so that the quantity

$$-\,\phi\,y = y - p'\bar{q} + \sigma\,\dot{p}'\beta$$

is actually variable. However, at the sample mean point, $\dot{p}'\beta = \iota'\beta = 1$, so that if we ignore any discrepancy between $\bar{y} = \overline{p'q}$ and $\bar{p}'\bar{q}$, we find that at the means, $\sigma = -\,\phi\,y$, which is Powell's original formulation.

4.5 Constant Elasticity of Demand Models

Models of consumer demand in which income and Cournot price elasticities are constant are probably the most widely used bases for empirical analysis of consumer expenditure patterns. Such a model is given by

$$(4.57)\qquad \log q = \alpha + \eta \log y + H \log p$$

where the parameters are the n x 1 vector α, the n x 1 income elasticity vector η, and the n x n Cournot price elasticity matrix H; algebraically

$$\log q_i = \alpha_i + \eta_i \log y + \sum_{j=1}^{n} \eta_{ij} \log p_j \qquad (i = 1,\ldots,n).$$

As is well known, constant elasticity of demand models cannot be rigorously deduced from maximization of a classical utility function, except for some pathological cases. For, unless all $\eta_i = 1$, high income elasticity goods will take a larger budget share as income rises with prices fixed. The weighted sum of income elasticities $\sum_i w_i \eta_i$ must then rise with income thus violating the Engel aggregation condition $\sum_i w_i \eta_i = 1$; see Wold and Juréen (1953, pp. 105-107).

Nevertheless, it is possible that (4.57) provides an adequate approximation, over the relevant range of variation of y and p, to demand behavior which would arise from maximization of classical utility. In most economic contexts, after all, a constant elasticity approximation is preferred to a constant slope approximation: log - linearity may be more realistic than linearity for Engel curves as it is for production functions. If so, it is plausible to impose classical restrictions on (4.57) as Stone (1953, pp. 275-278) proposed in his treatise on consumer expenditures in the United Kingdom. Suppose we define a general price index by

$$\log \pi = w' \log p,$$

w being the n x 1 average budget share vector. Then we may subtract and add $\eta \log \pi = \eta\, w' \log p$ on the right hand side of (4.57) to obtain

$$\log q = \alpha + \eta\,(\log y - \log \pi) + (H + \eta\, w') \log p$$

$$= \alpha + \eta \log (y/\pi) + H^* \log p; \tag{4.58}$$

algebraically

$$\log q_i = \alpha_i + \eta_i \log (y/\pi) + \sum_{j=1}^{n} \eta^*_{ij} \log p_j \qquad (i = 1,\ldots,n). \tag{4.59}$$

Here (y/π) is a measure of real income and $H^* = H + \eta w'$ is the Slutsky (i.e., utility-compensated) price elasticity matrix. The classical restriction which is to be imposed is that of homogeneity, (2.18f) $H^* \iota = 0$. This, as Stone (1953, p. 278) indicates, can be accomplished by replacing in each of the equations (4.59) the sum on the right by $\sum_{\substack{j=1 \\ j \neq k}}^{n} \eta^*_{ij} \log (p_j/p_k)$, with the numeraire good k being selected arbitrarily. Neither the Engel aggregation condition (2.15f) $w'\eta = 1$ nor the symmetry condition (2.17f) $(\hat{w} H^*)' = \hat{w} H^*$ are to be imposed, however; after all, η and H^* are taken as constant while w will vary.

This formulation remains uncomfortably rich in parameters, so that in practice the model is generally simplified even further by collapsing the price terms. A common procedure is to use only deflated income and deflated own-price as regressors (along with the intercept), deflation being by some conventional general price index, say π^*. Suppose that we subtract and add $\pi^*\eta^*_{ii} = -\pi^* \sum_{j=1, j\neq i}^{n} \eta^*_{ij}$ on the right of (4.59); we find

$$\text{(4.60)} \quad \log q_i = \alpha_i + \eta_i \log (y/\pi) + \eta^*_{ii} \log (p_i/\pi^*) + \sum_{\substack{j=1 \\ j\neq i}}^{n} \eta^*_{ij} \log (p_j/\pi^*).$$

Then it may be argued that since π^* is some weighted average of the p's, the sum on the right will be virtually zero and may be ignored, and similarly the distinction between π^* and π may be ignored, both to an approximation. This leaves the system as

$$\text{(4.61)} \quad \log q_i = \alpha_i + \eta_i \log(y/\pi^*) + \eta^*_{ii} \log(p_i/\pi^*) \qquad (i = 1,\ldots,n).$$

This at least is our interpretation, admittedly crude, of demand functions which relate quantities (strictly, deflated expenditures) to deflated income and deflated own-price. Such relations are fitted, e.g., by Houthakker (1965a). In his case, π^* is a Paasche price index: $\pi^* = \sum_j w^*_j (p_j/p^o_j)$, where the p^o_j are base period prices and the $w^*_j = p^o_j q_j/\sum_k p^o_k q_k$ are moving weights. Without loss of generality it may be assumed that base period prices are all unity, so that $\pi^* = \sum_j w^*_j p_j$. Then π^* and π differ only in being arithmetic and geometric averages, respectively, of the same set of prices.

In his own empirical work, Stone (1953, pp. 320-330) did not use (4.59) either. Though his description is a bit terse, it appears that he deflated income and prices by a fixed-weight consumer price index, and then dropped all but a few of the price terms: In the demand functions

> the price of the commodity in question divided by an index of all other prices (in practice the cost-of-living index adjusted where appropriate) appears in all cases, and wherever possible the relative prices, calculated in a similar way, of other commodities believed to be important complements or substitutes are included as well. At most four such complementary or substitute price relatives are included, and so the number of price relatives included in any one equation is at most five.
>
> Stone (1953, p. 328).

Since Stone was working with a classification of expenditures into about 50 categories, and using a sample of 19 observations, the need for some prior simplification of (4.59) was clear.[31]

4.6 Rotterdam School Demand Models

Coming full circle, we return to the logarithmic differentials which appeared in our initial investigation of the general features of complete sets of demand functions, Chapter 2. This approach to the formulation of consumer demand models, due to Barten and Theil, will be identified as that of the Rotterdam School.

In a remarkable paper, Barten (1964) not only presented for the first time the fundamental matrix equation of consumer demand theory and its solution, but also introduced the concept of "almost-additivity" (wherein off-diagonal elements of U are small, if not zero), implemented this by estimating a complete set of 14 consumer demand functions, incorporated stochastic prior information about the magnitudes of parameters, and utilized Zellner's "efficient estimation" procedure for fitting the multivariate regression model.

The functional form used in his study is that of (2.2g) above, rewritten here as

$$(4.62) \quad d\log q = \eta(d\log y - w'\, d\log p) + (H^{**} - \phi\, \eta\, w'\hat{\eta})\, d\log p.$$

The income elasticity vector η, the marginal-utility-of-income-compensated price elasticity matrix H^{**}, and the income flexibility ϕ, are taken as constant parameters. Differentials are replaced by first differences in the annual time series. The classical restrictions which should be imposed are any independent subset of those in (2.15g) - (2.18g). Specifically Barten (1964) takes Engel aggregation, symmetry, and homogeneity:

$$(4.63) \quad w'\eta = 1, \qquad (\hat{w}H^{**})' = \hat{w}H^{**}, \qquad H^{**}\iota = \phi\, \eta$$

giving his equations (2.26), (2.28), (2.27). However, exact imposition of these would be awkward since w is variable. Consequently, a further approximation is made, the sample mean value of the average budget share vector, $\bar{w}$, replacing w in (4.63).

Concern for a more convenient parameterization and for a sharper stochastic specification has led the Rotterdam School to a second model in which $\hat{w}\, d\log q$ rather than $d\log q$ itself appears as the dependent variable. Thus Theil (1965), Barten (1966), and Theil (1967) work with (2.2i) above, rewritten here as

$$(4.64) \quad \hat{w}\, d\log q = \mu(d\log y - w'\, d\log p) + (N - \phi\, \mu\, \mu')\, d\log p.$$

Now the marginal budget share vector μ, the marginal-utility-of-income-compensated price response matrix N, and ϕ are taken as constant parameters. Differentials are again replaced by differences. Once again Engel aggregation, symmetry, and homogeneity are imposed, this time in the form of (2.15i), (2.17i), and (2.18i), rewritten here as

$$(4.65) \quad \iota'\mu = 1, \qquad N' = N, \qquad N\iota = \phi\, \mu.$$

The constraints, it is apparent, have been expressed in terms of constants only. The constraints (4.65) are given as equations (6.17)-(6.18) in Theil (1965), as equations

(4.16)-(4.18) in Barten (1966, Chapter 2), and as equations (4.7), (4.8), (4.10) in Theil (1967, Chapter 6).

Empirical implementation of this model has focused on the special case in which direct additivity is assumed. In that case $N = \phi\ \hat{\mu}$, and (4.64) reduces to

$$(4.66) \qquad \hat{w}\ \mathrm{dlog}\ q = \mu\ (\mathrm{dlog}\ y - w'\ \mathrm{dlog}\ p) + \phi\ (\hat{\mu} - \mu\ \mu')\ \mathrm{dlog}\ p,$$

in which there are just n free parameters: the n - 1 independent elements of μ, and ϕ. The simplicity of (4.66) is strikingly apparent when it is expressed algebraically:

$$(4.67) \qquad w_i\ \mathrm{dlog}\ q_i = \mu_i\ (\mathrm{dlog}\ y - \textstyle\sum_j w_j \mathrm{dlog}\ p_j) + \phi\ \mu_i (\mathrm{dlog}\ p_i - \textstyle\sum_j \mu_j \mathrm{dlog}\ p_j) \qquad (i = 1,\dots,n).$$

In practice $(\mathrm{dlog}\ y - \sum_j w_j \mathrm{dlog}\ p_j)$ is approximated by $\sum_j w_j \mathrm{dlog}\ q_j$, which involves an error of the third order in the logarithmic differentials; see Barten (1966, p. 39) and Theil (1967, pp. 201-202, 222-223). The model remains nonlinear in the parameters and an iterative procedure for fitting it is employed.[32]

In a paper devoted to testing the classical restrictions, Barten (1967) works with a third model, (2.2h) above, rewritten here as

$$(4.68) \qquad \hat{w}\ \mathrm{dlog}\ q = \mu\ (\mathrm{dlog}\ y - w'\ \mathrm{dlog}\ p) + K\ \mathrm{dlog}\ p.$$

The constant parameters are now μ and the utility-compensated price response matrix K. Once again differentials are replaced by differences and $(\mathrm{dlog}\ y - w'\ \mathrm{dlog}\ p)$ by $w'\ \mathrm{dlog}\ q$. For the four-way breakdown of consumer expenditures, the equations of this model are estimated without constraints. The model is then reestimated subject to the classical restrictions of Engel aggregation, symmetry, and homogeneity, (2.15h), (2.17h), and (2.18h) above, rewritten here as

$$(4.69) \qquad \iota'\mu = 1, \qquad K' = K, \qquad K\iota = 0.$$

A comparison of goodness of fit before and after the constraints are imposed lends support to the validity of the classical restrictions. Focusing on the important Slutsky conditions, Barten concludes that symmetry is supported by the data, along with negativity of the utility-compensated own-price slopes. Parks (1969) comes to a similar conclusion in an application of the model to Swedish time series data, with n = 8.

If one is to assess the fruitfulness of the Rotterdam School models, it is important to recognize that no stigma attaches to their being approximate rather than exact. With the true utility function being unknown, there is after all no guarantee that any of the "exact" consumer demand models will be exact in fact. A differential formulation, quite possibly, provides an adequate approximation to utility-maximizing behavior over a range of conceivably true utility functions; this without being exactly appropriate for any particular one. Such robustness is naturally attractive.

The differential formulation appears to have expedited handling the classical restrictions and has stimulated a sharpening of the stochastic specification. As Parks (1969) remarks, first differencing may also aid in removing autocorrelation of disturbances. The models which have $\hat{W}$ dlog q as the dependent variable have an additional advantage of focusing attention on the phenomenon of main interest in many applications of consumer demand models -- variation in average budget shares.

One question that remains open is that of parameterization: which features of the demand functions ought to be treated as constant parameters? Barten's argument leading up to the selection of (4.64) is as follows; to maintain our notation scheme, we have resorted to some paraphrasing:

> In determining which form of demand function is most suitable for estimation, the problem is decide which terms in

$$dq = q_y\, dy + (\lambda\, U^{-1} - \lambda\, \lambda_y^{-1} q_y\, q_y' - q_y\, q')\, dp$$

should be treated as constant and which as variable. In our analysis, quantities, income, and prices are the essential variables and should therefore appear as variables in the demand equations, in their original form or in some transform. With respect to q_y, λU^{-1}, and $\lambda \lambda_y^{-1}$, some freedom remains. One may treat these magnitudes, or transforms thereof, as constants. Thus, for example, one might work with constant elasticities rather than constant partial derivatives. For time series analysis, the choice made will as a rule imply little difference from an empirical point of view. Given the fact that, in general, for the usual observation period of a year or less, income and prices change only slightly, it follows that virtually any form of demand function can be considered as a reasonable first approximation to the form which is optimal from the point of view of fit. In this study we shall therefore pay special attention to the possibility of imposing on the demand functions theoretical restrictions such as are contained in

$$p'q_y = 1, \quad \lambda U^{-1} = (\lambda U^{-1})', \quad \lambda U^{-1}p = \lambda \lambda_y^{-1}q_y.$$

Taking q_y, λU^{-1}, and $\lambda \lambda_y^{-1}$ as constants would then present the difficulty that constraints are imposed on the prices. Prices are, however, given, and on the present approach fundamentally independent, variables so that such constraints are inadmissible. We will therefore provide a transformation which makes it possible to handle the restrictions without this having restrictive consequences for the independent variables.

Barten (1966, pp. 27-28)

The ease with which the classical restrictions can be imposed is thus a prime consideration guiding the selection of parameters. (The relevance of the fact that y and p vary only slightly from year to year is not apparent: limited variability over the full sample would seem to be necessary to justify the approximation). A similar argument is offered by Theil; once again we have paraphrased at points:

> We shall work with constant parameters μ_i, ν_{ij} ... This constancy is restrictive, of course. It implies, as far as μ_i is concerned, that the optimal quantities are linear functions of income. Although this is probably not too serious when real income and relative prices are subject to moderate changes, it should be realized that equation (4.64) -- or, for that matter, any other form of demand equation -- is a Procrustean bed which fits empirical observations imperfectly. The main justification of (4.64) is its simplicity. We shall meet the μ's frequently in what follows; the analysis would be much more complicated if they were not constant but dependent on income and prices. Also, the symmetry condition on the ν's would be much more difficult to handle if they were not constant.
>
> ... The assumption of constant marginal budget shares is a simplifying approximation. In general, the μ's and also the ν's should be regarded as functions of income and prices ... However, the price of such a generalization is too heavy, since it would complicate the analysis considerably.
>
> Theil (1967, pp. 203-204)

It is clear that taking μ, N, and ϕ as constant does permit a convenient handling of the restrictions. This is especially so when the further assumption of additivity is made as in (4.66).

Nevertheless, the particular choice of constants may be questioned. Note first that constancy of N, taken strictly, ensures constancy of ϕ and μ: for, as shown previously, $\phi = \iota' N \iota$, and $\mu = \phi^{-1} N \iota$. The best-established empirical generalization on consumer behavior is what might be called the weakest version of Engel's law: "It is not the case that all income elasticities are unity." That is, average budget shares w vary with income y (prices p being fixed). The second and third Rotterdam School models (4.64) and (4.68) allow for this while maintaining simplicity of the Engel curves: they take the marginal budget shares μ as constant. This same feature -- constant marginal, but varying average, budget shares -- appeared in Stone's linear expenditure system. In that system, however, income flexibility ϕ was variable, being equal to $-(y - p'\gamma)/y$; in the present models ϕ is constant. Indeed in Stone's model, it was the variability of ϕ which provided the key component in the "explanation" of the variability of w: $w_i = (1 - |\phi|)w_i^* + |\phi|\mu_i$, where w_i^* is the ith subsistence budget share. It is a bit puzzling to find the Rotterdam School models having μ and ϕ constant. An explanation presumably will lie in the fact that these models are directly formulated in terms of changes in w.

These Rotterdam School models share with Stone's model not only linearity of the Engel curves, i.e. $p_i(\partial q_i/\partial y) = \mu_i$ independent of y for all i, but also $p_i(\partial q_i/\partial y)$ independent of p for all i. (As will be recalled, under the quadratic utility function, the Engel curves were also linear, but the slopes depended on prices). When such independence is taken together with direct additivity (as was done in the empirical applications of the second Rotterdam School model), a curious conclusion emerges if one ignores the approximative nature of the model. Goldberger (1969) shows that if utility is directly additive and marginal budget shares are independent of y and p, then the utility function must be of the Stone-Geary form

$$u = \sum_i \beta_i \log(q_i - \gamma_i).$$

If so, then the exact demand functions must be those of Stone's linear expenditure system.[33]

Finally, it may be of interest to examine the additivity assumption which was used in Barten's (1966) analysis of the n = 4 time series for the Netherlands but not used in Barten's (1967) analysis of essentially the same data. To test the additivity assumption formally requires measures of goodness of fit before and after additivity is imposed; these do not seem to appear on a comparable basis in the two publications. Recall however that additivity implies $K = \phi\ (\hat{\mu} - \mu\ \mu')$, that is that the matrix K is proportional to the matrix $\hat{\mu} - \mu\ \mu'$, the factor of proportionality being ϕ. Barten (1967, p. 83) reports the following estimates, obtained without an assumption of additivity:

$$\mu = (.1763 \quad .0884 \quad .4853 \quad .2500)'$$

$$K = \begin{pmatrix} -.1064 & .0219 & .0437 & .0408 \\ .0219 & -.0281 & .0026 & .0036 \\ .0437 & .0026 & -.0447 & -.0016 \\ .0408 & .0036 & -.0016 & -.0429 \end{pmatrix}.$$

Using the estimate of μ, we compute the estimate of $\hat{\mu} - \mu\mu'$:

$$\hat{\mu} - \mu\mu' = \begin{pmatrix} .1452 & -.0156 & -.0856 & -.0441 \\ -.0156 & .0806 & -.0429 & -.0221 \\ -.0856 & -.0429 & .2498 & -.1213 \\ -.0441 & -.0221 & -.1213 & .1875 \end{pmatrix}.$$

Determining whether the two estimated matrices are, apart from a proportionality factor, nonsignificantly different, is not trivial. We concentrate on the diagonal elements, and compute the ratios $\kappa_{ii}/[\mu_i(1 - \mu_i)]$ ($i = 1,\ldots,4$), each of which, on the additivity assumption employed in Barten's earlier work, is an estimate of the same parameter ϕ. These ratios are: -.73, -.35, -.18, -.23. These four estimates span a rather wide range; in terms of the income elasticity of the marginal utility of income, $\eta_{\lambda y} = \phi^{-1}$, the range is from -5.6 to -1.4. The dispersion is prima facie evidence against additivity; lacking access to the covariance matrix of the estimates of μ and K, we are unable to formalize this remark into a test. The most informative test, in any event, calls for a goodness of fit comparison.[34]

5
SUPPLEMENTARY REMARKS

This review of the utility underpinnings of complete sets of demand functions has ranged widely, although not exhaustively, over the contemporary literature on classical consumer demand theory. Reference has been made to stochastic specification and to empirical application, but the emphasis has been on an examination of the implications which various utility structures have for the functional form of complete systems of demand functions.

The analysis has thus been deterministic. Any demand system presented here will become, at best, merely the systematic component of an econometric model of consumer demand. For rigorous statistical inference to be undertaken, stochastic assumptions will have to be provided. While such assumptions will be specific to the form of demand system selected, there are general features that are likely to be shared by all consumer demand systems.

As is true in much econometric work, the systematic components in consumer demand models are generally interpreted as the conditional expectations of the dependent variables -- q or some transform thereof -- given the explanatory variables -- y and p or some transforms thereof. At least, this interpretation -- as Wold (1963) indicates -- provides the basic justification for least-squares fitting, which is, in one form or another, the estimation procedure used in virtually all empirical studies of consumer demand. But in view of the simultaneous determination of quantities, income, and prices in the economy, it is doubtful that the conditional expectations of q given y, p correspond to the structural demand functions which were the original referent of the classical theory. The coefficients in the conditional expectations reflect the average variation in quantities in response to the variations in incomes and prices in the population which generated the observed sample. But this population incorporates supply conditions which may not be permanent features of the economic landscape. Treating these coefficients as measures of the response in q to controlled changes in y and p, that is as measures of the responses to be expected when quite different supply conditions prevail, may well lead to serious error. In short, least-squares estimates of the consumer demand functions may be estimating mixtures of structural demand and supply functions. In econometric work on complete sets of demand functions, the tradition is to look this critical problem squarely in the face -- and then ignore it.[35]

Nonlinearity in the parameters is likely to be present in a complete set of consumer demand functions since the parameters in the demand function for one good are functionally related to those in the demand functions for all other goods. This, after all, is the force of the theoretical restrictions. Nonlinear regression programs are available, but questions of convergence remain. Such computations are considered by Stone (1954), Parks (1969), and Barten (1966, Chapters 5, 6); the last reference deals also with the nonlinearities which arise when parameters of the systematic demand functions appear again as parameters of the disturbance distribution.

The fact that the sum of expenditures p'q at each observation is equal to income y implies that there is an inherent interdependence among the contemporaneous disturbances in the n equations which make up the complete set. This implication is seen most directly in Stone's linear expenditure system. If, for empirical work, an n x 1 random disturbance vector ϵ is introduced, so that

$$\hat{p}\, q = \hat{p}\, \gamma + (y - p'\gamma)\, \beta + \epsilon \quad ,$$

then summing over the n equations gives

$$\iota'\hat{p}\, q = \iota'\hat{p}\, \gamma + (y - p'\gamma)\, \iota'\beta + \iota'\epsilon = y + \iota'\epsilon \ ,$$

since $\iota'\hat{p}\, \gamma = p'\gamma$ and $\iota'\beta = 1$. Because $\iota'\hat{p}\, q = p'q = y$, it follows that $\iota'\epsilon = 0$ so that the n elements of ϵ can hardly be independent random variables. In one form or another this interdependence arises in every complete set of demand functions. It calls for a generalized least squares estimation procedure, which may be complicated by the presumptive heteroskedasticity across equations, and by singularity of the disturbance covariance matrix: if $\iota'\epsilon = 0$, then $E(\epsilon\epsilon')$ cannot have rank n. Barten (1966, Chapter 5) attacks the problem in the setting of a Rotterdam School model; Parks (1969) develops the appropriate estimation procedures for several demand models, including Stone's linear expenditure system.

Time series provide the usual, although not exclusive, data base for estimation of complete sets of demand functions. Various authors have modified the demand functions to allow for changing tastes by means of time trends. For example, Stone (1954) makes β and γ linear functions of time, with coefficients to be estimated. The differential approximation models may bypass some of the time series problems by effectively differencing the series; Barten (1967), however, includes an implicit time trend in his differential formulation. Further work on the problem of autocorrelation is likely to build upon the extensions of Zellner's procedure for efficient estimation of multivariate regressions. Parks (1967) provides such an extension to handle both contemporaneous and serial correlation.

While the classical theory is articulated in terms of income, empirical work on complete systems of demand functions typically abstracts from the savings decision, by omitting savings from the list of goods and taking y to mean total consumption. The justification for this might rest on a two-stage model in which the consumer first allocates his income between savings and consumption, after which the classical theory applies to the allocation of consumption among its components. Statistical aspects of this are treated in Summers (1959) and Prais (1959).

Suppose that on grounds of theory and previous experience the class of admissible forms for a complete set of consumer demand functions has been narrowed down to two or three members. Suppose further that all the statistical problems have been resolved and that the two or three sets have been estimated. How is one to decide which form is best? In consumer demand analysis, as in econometrics generally, criteria for choosing among alternative functional forms are not well developed. A resolution of this awkward situation awaits a consensus on the uses to which the model will be put. In the interim, a pragmatic approach prevails, in which descriptive measures of goodness of fit can play a leading role. Theil (1965) proposed an information inaccuracy measure which concentrates on the success with which the models predict the composition of expenditures, i.e., the average budget shares w. This proposal is implemented in Theil (1967, pp. 241-245). Parks (1969) uses this measure along with more conventional indicators of goodness of fit.

FOOTNOTES

[1]We shall have frequent occasion to matricize vectors in this way. Let $a = (a_1, \ldots, a_n)'$ be an $n \times 1$ vector; then $\hat{a}$ will denote the $n \times n$ diagonal matrix whose ith diagonal element is a_i, namely

$$\hat{a} = \begin{pmatrix} a_1 & 0 & \ldots & 0 \\ 0 & a_2 & \ldots & 0 \\ \cdot & \cdot & & \cdot \\ \cdot & \cdot & & \cdot \\ 0 & 0 & \ldots & a_n \end{pmatrix}.$$

Such matrices have many special features. First, if $c = (c_1, \ldots, c_n)'$ is also an $n \times 1$ vector, then $\hat{a}\, c = \hat{c}\, a$ and $a'\hat{c} = c'\hat{a}$. Second, if $\iota = (1, \ldots, 1)'$ is the $n \times 1$ vector of 1's, then $\hat{a}\iota = a$ and $\iota'\hat{a} = a'$; incidentally $\hat{\iota}$ is the $n \times n$ identity matrix. Third, $\hat{a}$ is symmetric, $\hat{a}' = \hat{a}$. Fourth, being a diagonal matrix, $\hat{a}$ will commute with other diagonal matrices, e.g., $\hat{a}\,\hat{c} = \hat{c}\,\hat{a}$. When, as in the present context, the elements of a are nonzero, then $\hat{a}$ is clearly nonsingular. In that case, it is readily confirmed that $\hat{a}^{-1}a = \iota$ and $a'\hat{a}^{-1} = \iota'$. Finally if $b = \hat{c}\,a$, then $\hat{b} = \hat{c}\,\hat{a}$; if $b = c - a$, then $\hat{b} = \hat{c} - \hat{a}$.

[2]Our terminology follows that of Barten and Theil. Houthakker (1960a) uses the term "income flexibility" to refer to our $\lambda_y^{-1}\lambda = \phi\, y$. Frisch (1932, 1959) uses the term "money flexibility" to refer to our $\eta_{\lambda y}$.

[3]See Frisch (1959, p. 184) who introduces this type of response to prices in terms of elasticities.

[4]For a simple example, consider $u = \sqrt{q_1 q_2}$. It is not additive, but has an additive transform, namely $v = \log u = \frac{1}{2}\log q_1 + \frac{1}{2}\log q_2$. More generally, the relation (2.23) may be exploited in an attempt to find a $v(u)$ such that V is diagonal; see Samuelson (1947a, pp. 174-183).

[5]Samuelson (1965, pp. 795-796) remarks, "Let me merely express the hope here that some of the statistical users of these hypotheses [of additivity] will subject them to stringent empirical validation or refutation. In what sense do empirical calculations ... fail to approximate to these implications of direct additivity? To the economist this ... is the important question."

[6]In view of the assumption about the behavior of λ which underlies the use of $\eta_{\lambda y}$ as a welfare indicator, one may wonder why λ itself is not proposed as a welfare indicator. The explanation, apparently, is that λ is not even invariant under linear transformations: see Frisch (1932, p. 21).

[7]Consider the additive utility function $v = \frac{1}{2}\log q_1 + \frac{1}{2}\log q_2$ introduced in note 4. The demand functions are readily found to be

$$q_1 = \tfrac{1}{2}\, y/p_1 \qquad\qquad q_2 = \tfrac{1}{2}\, y/p_2\ ,$$

so that the indirect utility function is given by

$$v = \tfrac{1}{2} \log (\tfrac{1}{2} y/p_1) + \tfrac{1}{2} \log (\tfrac{1}{2} y/p_2)$$

$$= \log \tfrac{1}{2} + \log y - \log \sqrt{(p_1 p_2)}.$$

Then the marginal utility of income function is

$$\kappa = y^{-1} ,$$

the income slope of which is $\kappa_y = -y^{-2}$. The income elasticity of the marginal utility of income,

$$\eta_{\kappa y} = \kappa_y \, \kappa^{-1} y = -y^{-2} yy = -1,$$

does not vary with income. Its use as a welfare indicator is thus precluded.

[8]We are using the conventions that for two n x 1 vectors

$$a = (a_1,\ldots,a_n)' \qquad c = (c_1,\ldots,c_n)',$$

$$\left.\begin{array}{l} a < c \\ c > a \end{array}\right\} \text{ means } a_i < c_i \qquad (i = 1,\ldots,n),$$

$$\left.\begin{array}{l} a \leqslant c \\ c \geqslant a \end{array}\right\} \text{ means } a_i \leqslant c_i \qquad (i = 1,\ldots,n).$$

[9]This interpretation of its parameters suggests that the Stone-Geary functional form may be useful in contexts other than the allocation of consumer expenditures. In an empirical study of the work disincentives of the negative income tax, Leuthold (1968) uses the utility function

$$u = b \log (L - \bar{L}) + (1-b) \log (Y - \bar{Y}),$$

where L = hours of leisure, Y = disposable income, b is a parameter (measuring relative marginal valuation of L and Y) as are $\bar{L}$ = minimum required leisure and $\bar{Y}$ = minimum required disposable income. In the no-tax-no-unearned-income situation, this function is maximized subject to the time-budget constraint

$$K = L + w^{-1}Y$$

where K = total hours available (e.g. 720 per month) and w = hourly wage rate. For less special situations, the constraint is appropriately modified. Constrained maximization yields a supply curve of labor (analogous to our demand functions), which is then estimated. Those estimates can be translated into estimates of b, $\bar{L}$, and $\bar{Y}$ whereupon the response of work effort to a radically different tax-transfer law may be projected. Some of the analysis in Christensen's (1967) study of savings and the rate of interest is based upon an intertemporal utility function which generalizes the CES functional form in the same manner as the Stone-Geary function generalizes the Cobb-Douglas functional form -- namely by introducing "minimum required quantities."

[10]It may be surprising to find $(\partial q_i/\partial p_j) < 0$ for all $i \neq j$. But what this says is that all goods are gross complements. On the Hicks-Allen definition, they will all be substitutes in the present model, since the utility function is directly additive; see Section 3.3 below.

[11]Alternatively, $\alpha \neq 0$ may be ruled out by the requirement that $q_i = q_i(y, p)$ be homogeneous of degree zero in y, p.

[12]In this argument we have ignored the sign conditions $\beta > 0$, $\gamma \geqslant 0$, $(q - \gamma) > 0$ which do not follow from the restrictions (2.15a) - (2.17a), but rather from subtler conditions such as the negativity of the utility-compensated own-price slope. In this connection see Stone (1954, pp. 514-515) and Pollak (1971). An alternative characterization of Stone's linear expenditure system is provided by Goldberger (1969) and could be deduced from Pollak (1971). If the utility is directly additive and the marginal budget shares are constant, then the utility function must be of the Stone-Geary form, in which case the demand functions are those of Stone's linear expenditure system.

[13]It may be surprising to have the marginal utility of income rising with prices, as is the case here since $(y - p'\gamma)^{-2}\gamma > 0$. But while a price increase reduces each dollar's command over goods, it also raises the marginal utility of the goods (by reducing their quantities). Cf.

Theil (1967, p. 208), "the marginal utility of income depends not only on how much one can buy for a dollar, but also on how many dollars one has." The conflict of forces was reflected in

$$(2.12) \quad \lambda_p = -\lambda q_y - \lambda_y q$$

in which the first term is (normally) negative and the second term positive. In the linear expenditure system the second term inevitably dominates.

[14]To relax this limitation, Stone (1965, pp. 275-276) suggests a "price-sensitive" variant of his system which however has not been empirically implemented. We have not checked to see if it can be obtained by a classical utility maximization process.

[15]For a detailed discussion of the classes of direct and indirect functions which produce "locally linear" Engel curves, see Pollak (1971).

[16]See Houthakker (1960, 1965b) and Samuelson (1965). Indirect additivity means that the indirect utility function can be expressed as $u^*(y, p) = \sum_i u^{*i}(y/p_i)$ with each $u^{*i}(\quad)$ being a function of only the corresponding y/p_i. After discarding the (irrelevant) constant term $\sum_i \beta_i \log \beta_i$, (3.16) has this structure.

[17]On this distinction, in general terms, see Gorman (1953).

[18]Our interpretation remains tenuous, however. A similar interpretation with similar problems suggests itself in any model in which the Engel curves are linear, as they are here. See Pollak (1971).

[19]Recall that $\lambda_{yy} > 0$ is a necessary condition for $\partial\eta_{\lambda y}/\partial y > 0$. In the present model,

$$\lambda_{yy} = \partial\lambda_y/\partial y = -\partial(p'B^{-1}p)^{-1}/\partial y = 0,$$

and

$$\partial\eta_{\lambda y}/\partial y = -(p'B^{-1}\alpha - y)^{-2}p'B^{-1}\alpha < 0.$$

The perverse behavior may also be seen in terms of

$$|\phi| = -\eta_{\lambda y}^{-1} = (p'B^{-1}\alpha - y)/y.$$

This is the ratio of infrabliss deficit to income; it is falling monotonically over the income range to which the model applies. (A measure which rises with income is the ratio of income to bliss income, $y/p'B^{-1}\alpha$.) A plot of λ against y with p given would show a straight line with slope $-(p'B^{-1}p)^{-1}$, in contrast with the hyperbolic curve described earlier.

[20]That all income elasticities are equal (and hence equal to 1) could also be discovered by setting $\beta_i = \beta_j$ in (4.19). Recall that the Cobb-Douglas special case of Stone-Geary utility had this property too. It also had all Cournot own-price elasticities equal to -1 and all Cournot cross-price elasticities equal to 0. These latter properties are absent in the present special case of direct addilog utility. From (4.20) we do see that Cournot cross-price elasticities depend only upon the good whose price is being changed (and not upon the good whose quantity is responding). Using also the rule $\sum_i w_i \eta_{ij} = -w_j$ we find that Cournot own-price elasticities may be written as

$$\eta_{ii} = (1-\beta)^{-1}(-1 + \beta w_i).$$

As noted by Pollak (1971), this special direct addilog utility function is a monotonic transformation of the constant elasticity of substitution production function.

That function is typically written $v = (\sum_i \delta_i x_i^{-\rho})^{-1/\rho}$;

setting $\delta_i = \alpha_i$, $x_i = q_i$, $-\rho = \beta$, we see indeed that

$v = (\sum_i \alpha_i q_i^{\beta})^{1/\beta} = u^{1/\beta}$.

[21]Duality relationships linking direct and indirect utility functions are mentioned by Houthakker (1960a, p. 245, n. 3) and explored in detail by Samuelson (1965).

[22]Note the omitted step. Since q = q(y, p) must be homogeneous of degree 0 in y, p, the same must be true of $u = u^*(y, p)$. Thus there is no loss of generality in writing an indirect utility function as a function of

$y/p_1, \ldots, y/p_n$ only. The additivity concept is introduced with respect to this latter, canonical, form.

[23]Our expression (4.36) is the correct version of equation (23) of Houthakker (1960a), which in the present notation would be read off as

$$\eta_{ii} + 1 = -(1 - w_i)(\eta_i - \eta_{\lambda y}).$$

That this is in error is most readily seen by considering the Cobb-Douglas case discussed in Section 3.6. That case is indirectly (as well as directly) additive and has $\eta_{ii} = -1$, $\eta_i = 1$, and $\eta_{\lambda y} = -1$.

[24]The general indirect additivity restrictions (4.35)-(4.36) may be checked out in the present indirect addilog model. As will be shown in the text, $\eta_{\lambda y} = -1 + \sum_k \beta_k w_k$; taking this together with (4.43)-(4.44) we have

$$\begin{aligned} \eta_{ii} + 1 &= -\beta_i + \beta_i w_i = -(1 - w_i)\beta_i \\ &= -(1 - w_i)\,[-1 + \textstyle\sum_k \beta_k w_k + (1 + \beta_i) - \sum_k \beta_k w_k] \\ &= -(1 - w_i)\,(\eta_{\lambda y} + \eta_i) \end{aligned}$$

in conformity with (4.36). Note the implicit interpretation of the parameter β_i -- it equals $\eta_{\lambda y} + \eta_i$. Continuing, in the indirect addilog model we compute

$$u^*_{jj} = (\partial u^*_j/\partial p_j) = (1 + \beta_j)\, p_j^{-2}\, w_j\, \lambda\, y$$

by means of (4.38), (4.39), and (4.41) (in the latter two equations replacing i by j). When this expression is inserted on the right of (4.35) we obtain, in view of (4.44),

$$(1 + \beta_j)\, w_j - w_j = \beta_j\, w_j = \eta_{ij}$$

in conformity with (4.35).

[25]Note that the necessary condition for $\eta_{\lambda y}$ to rise with income is satisfied. Differentiating the second line above (4.45) gives

$$\lambda_{yy} = y^{-2}\lambda \textstyle\sum_k (\beta_k - 1)^2 w_k.$$

With $y > 0$, $\lambda > 0$, $(\beta_k - 1)^2 > 0$, and $w_k > 0$, we find $\lambda_{yy} > 0$, as required.

[26]To conclude, a final remark on indirect additivity may be made. As indicated in note 20, the special direct addilog utility function $u = \sum_i \alpha_i q_i^\beta$ generates demand functions in which the cross-price elasticities η_{ij} ($i \neq j$) are independent of i. According to Houthakker's theorem cited above, this implies that utility is indirectly additive. That is, the preference ordering depicted by the directly additive function $u = \sum_i \alpha_i q_i^\beta$ must also be representable by an indirectly additive function. This function may be found explicitly. Inserting the demand functions $q_i = q_i(y, p)$ from (4.24) into the special direct addilog utility function $u = \sum_i \alpha_i q_i^\beta$, we find after some manipulation the indirect utility function

$$u^*(y, p) = \beta^{-1}[\sum_i (y/p_i)^{\beta(1-\beta)^{-1}} \gamma_i^{(1-\beta)^{-1}}]^{(1-\beta)}.$$

While $u^*(y, p)$ is not additive, it has a monotonic transform which is, namely

$$v^*(y, p) = (\beta\ u^*)^{(1-\beta)^{-1}} = \sum_i [(y/p_i)^{\beta(1-\beta)^{-1}} \gamma_i^{(1-\beta)^{-1}}].$$

Monotonically increasing transformations of indirect utility functions represent the same preference ordering, as an argument parallel to that used in our discussion of direct utility would show. Thus this $v^*(y, p)$ gives an indirectly additive representation of the same preference ordering for which $u = \sum_i \alpha_i q_i^\beta$ gave a directly additive representation. We have here a second example of a preference ordering which is both directly and indirectly additive; the Cobb-Douglas case was our first. A distinction lies in the fact that the Cobb-Douglas case had those features "simultaneously," while the present case has them "non-simultaneously"; see Samuelson (1965, pp. 793-795).

The marginal utility of income function $\kappa = \kappa(y, p)$ associated with $v^*(y, p)$ is

$$\kappa = \partial v^*/\partial y = \beta(1 - \beta)^{-1} y^{-1} v^* ,$$

whose slope with respect to income is

$$\kappa_y = \partial\kappa/\partial y = \beta(1 - \beta)^{-1} y^{-2} v^* (2 \beta - 1)(1 - \beta)^{-1}.$$

The income elasticity of the marginal utility of income is now

$$\eta_{\kappa y} = \kappa_y y \kappa^{-1} = (2 \beta - 1)/(1 - \beta),$$

which will be positive, zero, or negative depending on whether β exceeds, equals, or is less than, 1/2, but which is in any event independent of the level of income. As is to be expected when monotonic transformations are made, this $\eta_{\kappa y}$ differs from the $\eta_{\lambda y} = (\beta - 1)$ found for the special direct addilog utility function itself.

Finally, note that it is $\eta_{\kappa y}$ (the "welfare indicator" of the indirectly additive representation) and not $\eta_{\lambda y}$ (the "welfare indicator" of the directly additive representation), which must be referred to in the indirect additivity theorem (4.36). To check out (4.36) in the present special case, we recall from note 20 that $\eta_{ii} = (1 - \beta)^{-1}(-1 + \beta w_i)$ and $\eta_i = 1$ under special direct addilog utility, whence

$$\begin{aligned} \eta_{ii} + 1 &= (1 - \beta)^{-1}(-1 + \beta w_i) + 1 \\ &= - (1 - w_i) \beta (1 - \beta)^{-1} \\ &= - (1 - w_i) [1 + (2 \beta - 1)/(1 - \beta)] \\ &= - (1 - w_i) (\eta_i + \eta_{\kappa y}) \end{aligned}$$

as called for by (4.36).

[27] In that discussion, an intercept vector α appeared on the right hand side but was shown to drop out. To simplify matters we now omit it from the outset. In the same spirit we will neglect the additive time trend variable actually employed by Powell.

[28] As, of course, it is in Stone's system, where $\hat{q} + \phi\, y\, \hat{\beta}\, \hat{p}^{-1} = \gamma$. Indeed, as we have seen, Stone's system would follow directly from (4.48) as soon as we would impose exactly the general requirements of classical demand theory, without any special assumption of additivity.

[29] It may be objected that introducing prices into the utility function violates the idea of a preference ordering which is fixed in the face of income and price variation. To avoid this difficulty, we may explain (4.55) by saying that we have prior information that $\bar{q} - \sigma\, \bar{\hat{p}}^{-1}\beta = \gamma$, where γ is indeed a fixed parameter vector. Note incidentally that σ is at this stage just an unknown scalar.

[30] To be fair, all this is on our simplified version of Powell's model which ignored an additive time trend in the expenditure functions. This "time trend variable is introduced in the hope of allowing for shifts in consumers' tastes," Powell (1966, p. 663). Powell's own model has the term $t\,\alpha$ added to the right hand side of (4.56), t being the scalar variable measuring time and α being an $n \times 1$ parameter vector with $\iota'\alpha = 0$. To arrive at this requires that we add the term $t\, \hat{p}^{-1}\alpha$ to the right hand side of (4.55) in specifying the γ vector.

[31] First difference versions of the demand functions were fitted by Stone (1953) and Houthakker (1965a). In interpreting these one may appeal to the logarithmic-differential approximation approach referred to in Sections 2.2, 2.3; see also Section 4.6.

[32] Estimates of the model have been reported only for a four-way breakdown of consumer expenditures for the Netherlands. This lowering of the aspiration level may be attributed to a rising concern for providing an economic basis for the stochastic specification, especially as regards the disturbance variance-covariance matrix. See Barten (1966, Chapters 5, 6) and Theil (1967, Chapter 7).

[33]Suppose that it is also assumed that ϕ is constant. Then on a strict interpretation, we must conclude that the demand functions are of the Cobb-Douglas form $q_i = \mu_i(y/p_i)$ $(i = 1,\ldots,n)$. For if utility is Stone-Geary, then $\phi = -(y - p'\gamma)/y$, and this will be constant only if $\gamma = 0$, in which case the Cobb-Douglas case obtains. All income elasticities are then unity, and $\phi = -1$. This last result is given by Theil (1967, p. 204). He arrives there via a different route, attributed to McFadden, which also shows that constancy of N, ϕ, and μ (with no additivity restriction), taken strictly, implies that $\nu_{ij} = (1 + \phi)\, \mu_i\, \mu_j$ for all $i \neq j$. The moral to all this was pointed out by Theil (1967, p. 203): If the starting point is a formulation "in terms of first-order effects (infinitesimal changes), the implications of the demand equations should also be confined to first-order changes."

[34]Barten (1966, pp. 130-133) reports on the computations made under the additivity assumption. In the iterative procedure used to estimate (4.66), initial values are taken as $\phi = -.50$ and $\mu = (.21, .08, .36, .35)'$. These are obtained, respectively, from Frisch's suggestions that $\eta_{\lambda y} = -2$ for the median part of the population, and from the average income elasticities reported by Houthakker (1965a). After one round, which is as far as the iteration scheme is carried out, the estimates are $\phi = -.32$ and $\mu = (.21, .10, .50, .19)'$. The standard error given for this estimate of ϕ is .09, which gives some standard by which to judge the dispersion of the four previous estimates.

[35]Another, considerably less important, problem associated with the conditional expectation interpretation arises when the dependent variables are logarithmic transformations of quantities. This problem is discussed, in the context of production models, by Goldberger (1968).

REFERENCES

Allen, R. G. D. and A. L. Bowley (1935), Family Expenditure: A Study of its Variation, London: Staples Press.

Barten, A. P. (1964), "Consumer demand functions under conditions of almost additive preferences," Econometrica, Vol. 32, January-April, pp. 1-38.

Barten, A. P. (1966), Theorie en Empirie van een Volledig Stelsel van Vraagvergelijkingen, doctoral dissertation, Netherlands School of Economics, Rotterdam.

Barten, A. P. (1967), "Evidence on the Slutsky conditions for demand equations," Review of Economics and Statistics, Vol. 49, February, pp. 77-84.

Christensen, L. R. (1967), Saving and the Rate of Interest, doctoral dissertation, Department of Economics, University of California, Berkeley.

Frisch, R. (1932), New Methods of Measuring Marginal Utility, Beiträge zur Ökonomischen Theorie, Tübingen: J.C.B. Mohr.

Frisch, R. (1954), "Some basic principles of price of living measurements: a survey article," Econometrica, Vol. 22, October, pp. 407-421.

Frisch, R. (1959), "A complete scheme for computing all direct and cross demand elasticities in a model with many sectors," Econometrica, Vol. 27, April, pp. 177-196.

Geary, R. C. (1949), "A note on 'A constant-utility index of the cost of living'," Review of Economic Studies, Vol. 18, pp. 65-66.

Goldberger, A. S. (1968), "On the interpretation and estimation of Cobb-Douglas functions," Econometrica, Vol. 36, July-October, pp. 464-472.

Goldberger, A. S. (1969), "Directly additive utility and constant marginal budget shares," Review of Economic Studies, Vol. 36, April, pp. 251-254.

Goldberger, A. S. and T. Gamaletsos (1970), "A cross-country comparison of consumer expenditure patterns," European Economic Review, Vol. 1, Spring, pp. 357-400.

Gorman, W. M. (1953), "Community preference fields," Econometrica, Vol. 21, January, pp. 63-80.

Houthakker, H. S. (1953), "La forme des courbes d'Engel," Cahiers du Seminaire d'Econometrie, No. 2, pp. 59-66.

Houthakker, H. S. (1960a), "Additive preferences," Econometrica, Vol. 28, April, pp. 244-257.

Houthakker, H. S. (1960b), "The influence of prices and incomes on household expenditures," Bulletin of the International Institute of Statistics, Vol. 37, No. 2, pp. 3-16.

Houthakker, H. S. (1965a), "New evidence on demand elasticities," Econometrica, Vol. 33, April, pp. 277-288.

Houthakker, H. S. (1965b), "A note on self-dual preferences," Econometrica, Vol. 33, October, pp. 797-801.

Klein, L. R. and H. Rubin (1947), "A constant-utility index of the cost of living," Review of Economic Studies, Vol. 15, pp. 84-87.

Kloek, T. (1966), Indexcijfers: Enige Methodologische Aspecten, doctoral dissertation, Netherlands School of Economics, Rotterdam.

Leuthold, J. (1968), Formula Income Transfers and the Work Decision of the Poor: An Application of a Model of Work-Leisure Choice, doctoral dissertation, Department of Economics, University of Wisconsin.

Parks, R. W. (1966), An Econometric Model of Swedish Economic Growth 1861-1955, doctoral dissertation, Department of Economics, University of California, Berkeley.

Parks, R. W. (1967), "Efficient estimation of a system of regression equations when disturbances are both serially and contemporaneously correlated," Journal of the American Statistical Association, Vol. 62, June, pp. 500-509.

Parks, R. W. (1969), "Systems of demand equations: an empirical comparison of alternative functional forms," Econometrica, Vol. 37, October, pp. 629-650.

Pollak, R. A. (1971), "Additive utility functions and linear Engel curves," Review of Economic Studies, Vol. 38, October, pp. 401-414.

Powell, A. (1965), "Post-war consumption in Canada: a first look at the aggregates," Canadian Journal of Economics and Political Science, Vol. 31, November, pp. 559-565.

Powell, A. (1966), "A complete system of consumer demand equations for the Australian economy fitted by a model of additive preferences," Econometrica, Vol. 34, July, pp. 661-675.

Powell, A. A., T. V. Hoa, and R. H. Wilson (1968), "A multi-sectoral analysis of consumer demand in the post-war period," Southern Economic Journal, Vol. 35, October, pp. 109-120.

Prais, S. J. (1959), "A comment," Econometrica, Vol. 27, January, pp. 127-129.

Rajaoja, V. (1958), A Study in the Theory of Demand Functions and Price Indexes, Societas Scientarium Fennica: Commentationes Physico-Mathematicae XXI, Helsinki.

Russell, R. R. (1965), The Empirical Evaluation of Some Theoretically Plausible Demand Functions, doctoral dissertation, Department of Economics, Harvard University.

Samuelson, P. A. (1947a), Foundations of Economic Analysis, Cambridge: Harvard University Press.

Samuelson, P. A. (1947b), "Some implications of 'linearity'," Review of Economic Studies, Vol. 15, pp. 88-90.

Samuelson, P. A. (1965), "Using full duality to show that simultaneously additive direct and indirect utilities implies unitary price elasticity of demand," Econometrica, Vol. 33, October, pp. 781-796.

Somermeyer, W. H., J. G. M. Hilhorst, and J. W. W. A. Wit (1961), "A method for estimating price and income elasticities from time series and its application to consumers' expenditures in the Netherlands 1949-1959," Statistical Studies, No. 13, pp. 30-53.

Somermeyer, W. H. and J.W.W.A. Wit (1956), "Een 'verdeel'-model," Netherlands Central Bureau of Statistics.

Stone, R. (1953), The Measurement of Consumers' Expenditure and Behavior in the United Kingdom 1920-38, Volume I, Cambridge: Cambridge University Press.

Stone, R. (1954), "Linear expenditure systems and demand analysis: an application to the pattern of British demand," Economic Journal, Vol. 64, September, pp. 511-527.

Stone, R., ed. (1962), A Programme for Growth: 1. A Computable Model of Economic Growth, London: Chapman and Hall.

Stone, R., ed. (1964), A Programme for Growth: 5, The Model in Its Environment, A Progress Report, London: Chapman and Hall.

Stone, R. (1965), "Models for demand projections," pp. 271-290, in C. R. Rao, editor, Essays on Econometrics and Planning, Oxford: Pergamon.

Stone, R. (1966), *Mathematics in the Social Sciences and Other Essays*, London: Chapman and Hall.

Stone, R., A. Brown, and D. A. Rowe (1964), "Demand analysis and projections for Britain, 1900-1970: a study in method," pp. 200-225, in J. Sandee, editor, *Europe's Future Consumption*, Amsterdam: North-Holland.

Summers, R. (1959), "A note on least squares bias in household expenditure analysis," *Econometrica*, Vol. 27, January, pp. 121-126.

Theil, H. (1961), *Economic Forecasts and Policy*, Second Edition, Amsterdam: North-Holland.

Theil, H. (1964), *Optimal Decision Rules for Government and Industry*, Amsterdam: North-Holland.

Theil, H. (1965), "The information approach to demand analysis," *Econometrica*, Vol. 33, January, pp. 67-87.

Theil, H. (1967), *Economics and Information Theory*, Amsterdam: North-Holland.

Watts, H. W. (1967), "The Iso-Prop index: an approach to the determination of differential poverty income thresholds," *Journal of Human Resources*, Vol. 2, Winter, pp. 3-18.

Wold, H.O.A. (1963), "On the consistency of least squares regression," *Sankhya*, Series A, Vol. 25, Part II, July, pp. 211-215.

Wold, H.O.A. and L. Juréen (1953), *Demand Analysis*, New York: John Wiley & Sons.